The International Indigenous Recognition of Prior Learning (RPL) Practitioner Manual

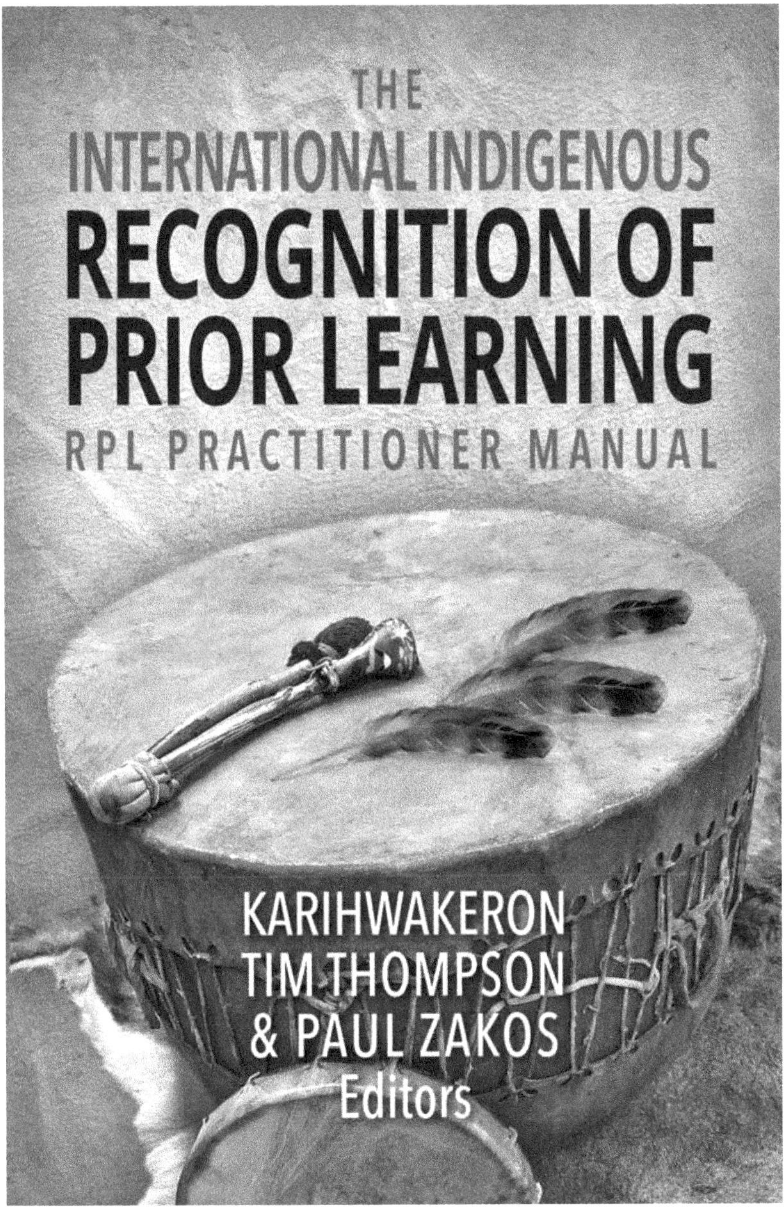
THE
INTERNATIONAL INDIGENOUS
RECOGNITION OF
PRIOR LEARNING
RPL PRACTITIONER MANUAL
KARIHWAKERON
TIM THOMPSON
& PAUL ZAKOS
Editors

Epic Press

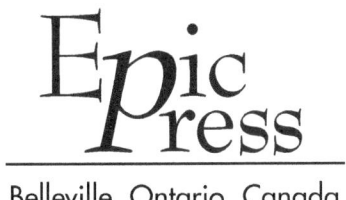

Belleville, Ontario, Canada

THE INTERNATIONAL INDIGENOUS RECOGNITION OF
PRIOR LEARNING (RPL) PRACTITIONER MANUAL

Copyright © 2021, The International Indigenous RPL Collective

All Rights Reserved. No part of this publication may be reproduced, stored in a retrieval system or transmitted in any form or by any means—electronic, mechanical, photocopy, recording or any other—except for brief quotations in printed reviews, without the prior permission of the author.

Cataloguing data available from Library and Archives Canada

ISBN: 978-1-4600-1256-7
LSI Edition: 978-1-4600-1257-4
E-book ISBN: 978-1-4600-1258-1

(E-book available from the Kindle Store, KOBO and the iBooks Store)

To order additional copies, visit:
www.essencebookstore.com

For more information, please contact:
Karihwakeron Tim Thompson
Chair, Board of Directors, RPL Collective
centreoftheuniverse1@gmail.com

Guardian Books is an imprint of *Essence Publishing,* a Christian Book Publisher dedicated to furthering the work of Christ through the written word.
For more information, contact:
20 Hanna Court, Belleville, Ontario, Canada K8P 5J2
Phone: 1-800-238-6376 • Fax: (613) 962-3055
Email: info@essence-publishing.com
Web site: www.essence-publishing.com

*This manual is dedicated to Carlos Sebastian,
who passed away in 2014. Carlos was a founding member
of the International Indigenous RPL Collective. He was a
fearless and impassioned colleague, a champion of social justice
and human rights, who worked tirelessly and selflessly.
His spirit will live forever in our work and in our hearts.*

Table of Contents

PREFACE. 11
ACKNOWLEDGEMENTS. 13
INTRODUCTION TO THE MANUAL 17
Purpose. 17
How to Use This Manual 18
Intellectual Property and Ownership 18
Assumptions of the Manual. 19
Overview of the Modules—Quality Assurance in Indigenous RPL 20
Module Format 20
Structure of the Manual 21

MODULE I: The Relationship Between Indigenous Knowledge, Adult Learning Principles, RPL, and Portfolio Development . . . 23
   Introduction. 23
   Module Outcomes 23
Indigenous Knowledges, Identities, and the Legacy of Oppression 24
Introduction to the First Nations Holistic Learning Model 32
Introduction to Adult Learning Theory and Practice 32
The Role of the International Indigenous RPL Practitioner/Advisor . . 35
Competencies of the Advisor—The Role of RPL and
Adult Learning Principles. 36
   Adult Learning Theory and Practice. 36
Malcolm Knowles and Andragogy. 36
     Concept of the Learner. 36

Previous Learning Experiences 37
Readiness to Learn 38
Orientation to Learning 38
Indigenous RPL Practitioner Responsibilities 38
PLAR and Portfolio-Assisted Assessment 39
Context 39
Definition 40
Key Purposes of PLAR 41
Benefits of PLAR 41
Assessment Methods 43
Adult-Centred Assessment Methods 43
PLAR and Portfolio Development 44
Portfolio-Assisted PLAR 44
PLAR and Adults in Transition 45
What is a Portfolio? 45
What are the Components of a Portfolio? 46
What are the Steps in the Portfolio Development/Evaluation Process? . . 47
Additional Benefits of Compiling a Portfolio 48

MODULE II: The Role of RPL in Addressing Issues of Social Justice, Inequality, Oppression, and Educational Reform. 49

Introduction 49
Module Outcomes 49

CANADA

Strengthening Indigenous Cultures and Languages, Promoting Healing and Social Justice in Canada 50
Conversations Toward Reconciliation and Healing 50
The Wisdom of the Old People 51
Where We Come From 52
Foundational 52
History of Truth and Reconciliation Commissions 55
Canada and the TRC 56

SOUTH AFRICA

Using the Recognition of Prior Learning (RPL) as a Tool for Social Action in South Africa 58

TABLE OF CONTENTS

Approach to Education Practice 59
The Recognition of Prior Learning (RPL) 60
Activism as the Foundational Module............................ 63
Reflections on the Module 72
Reflections on the Work of the Workers' College: As an Organization
for Social Change in a Society Trying to Renew Itself............... 72

CHILE
Breaking Down Barriers and Strengthening Indigenous Culture
and Language—The Role of PLAR 74
Mapuche Cosmovision and Circle of Life........................ 79

MODULE III: Training International Indigenous RPL Practitioners 81
Introduction 81
Module Outcomes 81

Key Competencies of the Indigenous RPL Practitioner 82
    Creating a Portfolio Process to Complement Indigenous Teachings:
    Basic Principles 82
Scale 84
Collecting Evidence to Support Competence..................... 84
Self-Assessment Scale 86
RPL Advisor Competences and Performance Indicators............ 87
Roles and Responsibilities—Indigenous RPL Advisor............... 87
Sample of a Possible Portfolio Framework 92

MODULE IV: Examples of Diverse Indigenous Applications of RPL and Portfolio Development..................... 93
Introduction 93
Module Outcomes 93

Creating a Portfolio Process to Complement Indigenous Teachings—
Principles and Processes 94
    The Canoe of Life... 94
Coast Salish Canoe of Life Model of Portfolio 101
Long House 103
The Igloo of Life 119

The International Indigenous RPL Practitioner Manual

MODULE V: Indigenous Knowledge and Quality Assurance—Assessing Your Institution or Program's Level of Integration of Indigenous Knowledge Using the Benchmarks of Best Practice Developed by the Collective 125
    Introduction 125
    Module Outcomes 125
Context for the Institutional Self-Evaluation Process 126
Introduction to the Institutional Self-Assessment Process 127
Performing the Informal Institutional Self-Assessment 128
Preparing a Final Report—Suggested Framework 129
Institutional/Organizational Informal Self-Assessment Roles and Responsibilities Related to Implementing Culturally Respectful Indigenous Knowledge Systems and Programs 130
    1. Principle—Emotional/Feeling 130
    2. Principle—Mental/Thinking 131
    3. Principle—Physical/Doing 132
    4. Principle—Spiritual/Seeing 133
Summary 134

APPENDIX A: United Nations Declaration on the Rights of Indigenous Peoples 137

APPENDIX B: World Indigenous Nations Higher Education Consortium (WINHEC) 139
WINHEC Goals 139

APPENDIX C: The International Indigenous RPL Collective 141
Vision 141
Mission 141
Objectives 142

APPENDIX D: Serving Indigenous Learners and Their Communities 143
Institutional Profile 143
Reflective Questions 143
Lessons Learned 144

Preface

The International Indigenous Recognition of Prior Learning (RPL) practitioner manual provides Indigenous peoples with practical portfolio development models and applications to document prior learning through an Indigenous lens. Indigenous cultures, customs, and perspectives are the foundation for the development of this approach to recognize and validate an Indigenous individual's learning journey.

The models support Indigenous peoples' efforts to document their knowledge, skills, and abilities in ways that they can see themselves fulfilling their responsibilities to family, community, and their Nations, enabling them to identify the next steps on their learning journey. The portfolio process empowers individual learners and by extension has the effect of strengthening Indigenous peoples' cultures, traditional teachings, languages, and self-determination.

The manual provides examples from Indigenous peoples of South Africa, the Coast Salish, the Haudenosaunee, the Inuit in Canada, and the Mapuche in Chile. To respect Indigenous knowledge and ways of knowing, this manual is intended to inform RPL processes led by Indigenous people, Indigenous practitioners, and Indigenous organizations.

Acknowledgements

This manual is based on extensive PLA and adult learning practice over a period of three and a half decades in both Indigenous and mainstream settings. We are indebted to the growing body of PLAR practitioners and adult learners internationally who have chosen to implement the portfolio development process for a variety of purposes. These uses include personal and cultural development, education, training, and employment.

PLA was introduced in the USA in the mid-1970s by the Council for Adult and Experiential Learning (CAEL) to help experienced adults access formal study at the post-secondary level and as a way to formally recognize learning that had taken place outside of formal settings. Gradually PLA practice spread to other countries, such as the UK, Canada, and South Africa. Its application broadened to include credit and recognition for workplace skills and knowledge to enhance employability and enable mobility within occupations.

Over the past three decades the assessment of prior learning has been described using a variety of terms—initially as Prior Learning Assessment (PLA) and eventually as Prior Learning Assessment and Recognition (PLAR) and more recently as the Recognition of Prior Learning (RPL). All three acronyms are used in various sections of the manual.

In 1985 PLA was introduced to Indigenous learners enrolled in a two-year social service worker diploma program at First Nations Technical Institute (FNTI) in collaboration with Loyalist College in Belleville, Ontario. The institute is an Indigenously owned and operated college located on the Tyendinaga Mohawk Territory in the province of Ontario. This was one of the first applications of PLA principles as an integral component of an Indigenous post-secondary program in which Indigenous knowledge and cultural teachings were key components of the curriculum.

In 2003 a training manual for PLA advisors was developed by the PLA Department of FNTI for South Africa's Manufacturing, Engineering and Related Services Education and Training Authority (MERSETA). This manual was used to train PLA advisors for the MERSETA in several locations throughout South Africa. The manual drew extensively on existing mainstream PLA practice. It also included a section entitled "Recognizing the Importance of Cultural Knowledge and Language Skills in the Portfolio Development Process."

From 2004 to 2005, a culturally based PLA initiative by the federally (Canada) funded Indigenous Peoples Partnership Program (IPPP) was implemented in Chile between Taiñ Adkimn, a community based Mapuche organization and FNTI. In 2006 a similar portfolio-based initiative also funded by the Canadian IPPP took place between FNTI, Taiñ Adkimn, and the School for Indigenous (Quechua) Governance in Ecuador.

In 2010 FNTI partnered with Nunavut Arctic College to develop and implement another federally funded PLA initiative which integrated PLA, portfolio development, and adult learning principles with Inuit teachings.

This manual draws heavily on those experiences as well as best practices from mainstream PLA as the basis for some of its content. It applies the learning from those experiences in a more in-depth and purposeful way to create a model of Indigenous PLA practice that we hope will be useful to other Indigenous nations around the world. Our intent is to add to the practice that has taken place and to deepen its impact and expand its reach as a practical tool to strengthen Indigenous culture and languages, including self-government and Indigenous control over the content, delivery, and evaluation of Indigenous education and training and as an antidote to the social injustice and racism that continues to contribute to the inequities of the societies in which Indigenous peoples live.

The creation of this manual has been made possible by the commitment and dedication of a relatively small but growing group of people

ACKNOWLEDGEMENTS

who believe strongly in the power of PLAR and portfolio development as a force for social justice and educational change for Indigenous learners and their communities.

In the spring of 2009 at the 20th annual PLAR conference hosted by FNTI, a steering committee was formed to explore the development of an International Indigenous Recognition of Prior Learning (RPL) Collective. Members of that committee included María Hueichaqueo, Pedro Valenzuela, directors; Taiñ Adkimn, Santiago, Chile; Luis Maldonado, director, School for Indigenous Governance, Quito, Ecuador; Jennifer Archer, program manager, Nunavut Arctic College; Kessie Moodley, director, Workers' College, Durban, South Africa; Nqabomzi Gawe, vice-chancellor, Durban, University of Technology, South Africa; Karihwakeron Tim Thompson; Diane Hill; Banakonda Kennedy-Kish Bell; Carlos Sebastian and Paul Zakos, FNTI. Dr. Malcolm Day, Derby University in the UK, has also been a strong supporter of the Collective for many years as has Yellowhead Tribal College in Edmonton, Alberta. The Aboriginal Department of Vancouver Island University, headed by Sharon Hobenshield, has been instrumental in expanding Indigenous PLAR practice and supporting the growth and development of the Collective.

The foundation for the Collective is the United Nations Declaration on the Rights of Indigenous Peoples, Articles 13, 14 (Appendix A) and the Mission and Vision of the World Indigenous Nations Higher Education Consortium (WINHEC) (Appendix B). A draft mission, vision, and statement of objectives (Appendix C) for the Collective were shared with approximately 100 conference delegates at the 20th annual conference, which included five members of the Aboriginal Circle of the Ontario Public Services Employees Union (OPSEU). Warren "Smokey" Thomas, OPSEU President, has been a steadfast supporter of the Collective and prior learning from the beginning.

The majority of delegates strongly endorsed the concept of the Collective and its draft mission, vision, and objectives. Many delegates offered concrete suggestions for strengthening the Collective.

The composition of the organization has changed somewhat since the original meeting in 2009. New members have been added and regular planning meetings have taken place with the overarching goal of formalizing the organization. In December 2016, a two-day strategic planning session, facilitated by James Reid, took place in Belleville, Ontario. Emerging from that meeting was the formation of a board of directors and a commitment to become incorporated as a Canadian non-profit organization. Incorporation took place in January of 2017. Officers of the board include President Karihwakeron Tim Thompson, Vice-President Sharon Hobenshield, and Secretary-Treasurer Glen Brouwer. Board members include Pedro Valenzuela, Banakonda Kennedy-Kish Bell, Heather Green, James Reid, Mark Gallupe, and Paul Zakos.

The board agreed to create this manual as a tool to assist in the training of international Indigenous RPL practitioners. It was also decided that the Collective would host a conference in 2021 to highlight the manual and to share it with others.

It is important to acknowledge the critical role played by our colleague Lynn Wilson in helping to create the first draft of this manual two years ago. Lynn's organizational skills and her creativity in developing the structure and format for the original manual have been invaluable. We would have been lost without her!

Introduction to the Manual

Purpose

This manual has been created to train international Indigenous recognition of prior learning (RPL) practitioners by equipping them with the skills, knowledge, and understanding needed to support Indigenous adult learners in meeting their personal, cultural, education, training, and employment goals. It identifies and discusses the critical processes that must be in place to support Indigenous learners interested in pursuing a variety of learning goals. It does so by implementing RPL processes which respect and honour cultural teachings and are integrated with the teachings of the Indigenous cultures of the participants.

The manual also outlines essential elements that must be in place to assist individuals pursuing their learning goals and includes the support and resources needed to assist learners throughout the entire process.

The portfolio development process can represent a fresh start for many adults who otherwise might not be willing to take up the challenges and risks associated with reviewing and reflecting on significant and sometimes painful learning events in their lives. Many learners may have dropped out of school early while others may have experienced problems affecting their families or employment.

The relationship between the Indigenous RPL practitioner and the adult learner is central to enhancing learner self-confidence and widening the possible uses of the portfolio depending upon the goals and aspirations of the learner. The interaction between the practitioner and learner is a key building block for learner success. The significance of establishing a supportive, positive relationship based on mutual respect, trust and unconditional acceptance of the language, culture, and life circumstances of the learner cannot be understated. Developing strategies and processes that encourage adult learners to be active partners in the planning process and ultimately taking the lead are also key components of this manual. The various dimensions of the practitioner's role are outlined in detail, and they include advocating, educating, counselling, mentoring, and collaborating with the adult learner.

How to Use This Manual

This manual is intended to be a user-friendly guide and a resource for training international Indigenous RPL practitioners. It contains a balance of PLAR and adult learning theory and demonstrates with examples the application of that theory to a portfolio-based process which is rooted in Indigenous knowledge and ways of knowing. Our hope is that you will use the material in ways that best meet your needs and the context in which you are working and interacting with Indigenous learners and their communities. We view the manual as a work in progress and invite you to join with us in our collective efforts to implement the mission and vision of the International Indigenous RPL Collective.

Intellectual Property and Ownership

PLAR is not owned by one entity, and its philosophy and practice as espoused by the Collective is based on the nurturing and building of relationships with other like-minded individuals and groups based on respect and transparency.

PLAR as practised by members of the Collective builds on the strengths and needs of Indigenous communities and includes the uses of cultural teachings and traditional knowledge as key components. It is in the spirit of mutual cooperation and collective action and consciousness raising that this work is shared and hopefully enhanced by its application in a variety of Indigenous nations and their communities worldwide.

INTRODUCTION TO THE MANUAL

Assumptions of the Manual

This manual is based on the firm belief that people learn best by doing and reflecting upon what happened. Other assumptions about learning also support the content, structure, and processes described on the pages that follow. They include the following:

As an Indigenous RPL practitioner, you can help shape the content, process and tools offered in this manual by your own experiences, values, and views of adult learners, the learning process, counselling, advocating, and cultural teachings.

You will bring into this activity those resources and ideas that enable you to effect change in the areas that most fit your experiences, values, skills and attitudes, and the ways in which you may have interacted with adults in the past. Generally you will respond to what is familiar to you, and directions in this manual are meant to be taken as suggestions and alternatives. You may also have other strategies and techniques for helping Indigenous adults meet their personal, cultural, education, training and employment goals that have worked for you in the past. We urge you to draw upon them as well and to share them with your colleagues.

The activities and resources described in this manual are part of a growing body of theory and practice related to helping adults achieve their personal, cultural, education, training, and employment goals. Effective advising is based on flexibility, clarity, and relevance to the needs and circumstances of the adult learner as an Indigenous person.

The information and processes in this manual may perform other important functions in addition to those outlined above. First, we hope that they will strengthen your commitment as an advocate for Indigenous adult learners and that you will join with colleagues in similar positions to continue to provide high quality advising services to Indigenous adults as they pursue personal, cultural, employment, education, and training goals. The activities described in this manual are intended to be participatory and action oriented. It is our desire to assist you to become an effective and competent Indigenous RPL practitioner by providing you with the best resources and support in your advisory role.

A skilled and caring advisor can have a significant and lasting impact on an adult learner's future hopes and aspirations. In this regard another goal of this manual is to encourage and support the development of the skills, knowledge, and attitudes needed to ensure that this will in fact be the case. We hope that you will agree with our views and make the experience worthwhile and meaningful for both yourself and the adult learner in order to improve the quality of learning and development of individuals as proud and confident Indigenous people.

Overview of the Modules—Quality Assurance in Indigenous RPL

The modules which follow have been designed to demonstrate how Indigenous knowledge, adult learning, and RPL have been integrated within a culturally respectful framework. This approach is illustrated by means of examples of RPL and adult learning practices in Canada, South Africa, and Chile. In addition, generic principles of Indigenous RPL practice have been identified and implemented with three separate Indigenous cultural groups. Arising from that practice has been the creation of two self-assessment tools aimed at identifying best practice in international Indigenous RPL.

The first example is a portfolio-based self-assessment process for Indigenous RPL practitioners. The second example is a self-evaluation process for educational institutions and programs to determine their level of integration of Indigenous knowledge using benchmarks and performance criteria. This is also a portfolio-based process enabling institutions and programs to identify strengths and gaps in service to Indigenous learners and communities.

Module Format

Each module begins with an introduction to the module which explains its purpose followed by a list of intended outcomes. One of the key characteristics of the manual is its adult-centred and collaborative approach, stressing mutual learning and sharing rather than a more rigid, conventional, teacher-centred approach. This process encourages the Indigenous RPL practitioner to work with learners and their communities rather than teaching them, helping them to identify needs, abilities, and strengths using cultural teachings. This requires developing a more sensitive, empathetic approach, trusting the adults' capabilities, building on

INTRODUCTION TO THE MANUAL

their strengths, skills, and interests, while helping them to overcome the obstacles and barriers that may be preventing them from moving forward in their lives.

It is our intent that Indigenous RPL practitioners will use a combination of one-to-one and group activities to assist learners, treating them with dignity and respect. It is our belief that adults learn best by doing. It is the intent of this manual to engage with learners, helping them explore who they are and where they are going using cultural teachings, culturally based RPL, and adult learning principles and processes. These components are central to this manual and imbedded in the various modules.

Structure of the Manual

The introductory section, **Module I**, outlines the relationship between Indigenous knowledge, adult learning theory and practice, RPL, and portfolio development. The module serves as the foundation for the other four modules.

Module II describes the role of RPL and portfolio development in addressing long-standing issues of social justice, inequality, oppression, and educational reform in Canada, South Africa, and Chile.

Module III highlights the key functions of RPL practitioners in relation to the roles of advisor and assessor. It integrates principles drawn from mainstream practice with competencies of Indigenous RPL practitioners using examples drawn from three models of Indigenous RPL practice. This module also contains a portfolio-based self-assessment component enabling Indigenous practitioners to compare their skills and knowledge to those of the Indigenous RPL practitioner.

Module IV provides examples of the application of the portfolio development process with cultural teachings drawn from three Indigenous cultures. The three processes are the "Canoe of Life," "The Longhouse," and The Igloo of Life." This module also articulates a set of generic guidelines which may be used in the creation of a portfolio development process for international use with a variety of Indigenous cultures.

Module V focuses on benchmarks of quality assurance in delivering educational services to Indigenous learners. It outlines an evidence-based, self-assessment process to assist educational institutions and programs to determine the quality of their programs and services for Indigenous learners. A portfolio of evidence is gathered, enabling the institution or program to measure its services to Indigenous learners against the benchmarks and their performance criteria.

MODULE I

The Relationship Between Indigenous Knowledge, Adult Learning Principles, RPL, and Portfolio Development

Introduction

This module identifies basic teachings supporting Indigenous cultures. It describes various elements that comprise an Indigenous world view, and it integrates this knowledge within a larger framework encompassing adult learning theory and practice, including prior learning assessment (PLA) and portfolio development. The overarching goal is to demonstrate how these three components combine to create a powerful and practical Indigenous RPL process that cuts across cultures internationally.

Module Outcomes

Upon successful completion of this module participants will be able to:

- Describe four components that comprise an Indigenous world view and how they can be integrated into a portfolio development process.
- Identify four key principles of the process of andragogy as articulated by Malcolm Knowles.
- Define PLAR and portfolio development—outline purposes, benefits, and uses for both.
- Outline the steps involved in the portfolio development process.
- Identify adult-centred, competency-based assessment methods.
- Describe five key principles for documenting prior learning.

Indigenous Knowledges, Identities, and the Legacy of Oppression—*Karihwakeron Tim Thompson*

I have seen terms such as "traditional ecological knowledge" or "traditional environmental knowledge" applied in scholarly papers to classify, examine, understand, and debate matters relating to Indigenous knowledge. My purpose here is not to engage in that debate because I want to talk about my grandma.

My grandmother always had various herbs drying in the pantry. There were different leaves, grasses, roots, fungi, even animal parts. She would make various salves to be utilized when someone was in need and different teas which could be consumed to address various ailments.

On one occasion in my youth, Grandma and I were outside when I noticed a plant which I recognized from the pantry. As I went to pick it, Grandma stopped me and told me I couldn't just pick that medicine plant without giving something back. She told me that I should give some silver to the plant in exchange for its healing gift. She handed me a dime, and I put it next to the plant.

Often, Indigenous knowledge is turned into a commodity. In the brief story above, the particular use of the plant is the piece that is often identified as Indigenous knowledge. It is true that Indigenous knowledge consists of observations and practices which are unique to our cultures and environments. However, Indigenous knowledge is also holistic. It derives from thousands of years of lived experience, connected to a particular land base and ecology, and it is expressed through our languages, our cultural practices, values, beliefs, and the relationships we maintain with one another and to the natural world.

No matter where one travels among Indigenous peoples, there are origin stories. Often, there is a grand story about how humans and the natural world came to be, with more specific stories about how particular nations emerged and how the people came to know the world around us. These origin stories tell us where we came from, the journey we have here on Mother Earth, and begin to give us an understanding of the purpose(s) we are to serve. Symbols of our origin story and our understanding of the world find their way into designs on our clothes, our pottery, and even in the structure of our longhouses.

MODULE I

Origin stories begin to tell us about the relationships we are to have with each other and with the world around us. By understanding our origins and our relationships, we can make the personal connections necessary to begin to answer some essential questions:

"Who am I?"

"Where do I come from?"

"Why am I here? What is my purpose?"

"Where am I going? What is my future?"

"What are my gifts/talents?"

"How do I contribute to others around me?"

"How can I make a difference?"

When we know where we come from and we understand our roles and responsibilities, we are then mandated with manifesting this knowledge through our behaviours. Indigenous knowledge includes the ceremonies we practice in our lodges, roundhouses, and longhouses, and the rituals we conduct when we ask the animals or medicines to share their gifts with us. However, it also includes the way we speak to each other, the way we carry ourselves, the way we prepare to welcome children and grandchildren in the world, and the way we support our elders in our families and communities.

Indigenous languages provide the primary means of expressing our world views. Our languages express unique words and concepts which arise from our thousands of years of lived experience, connected to a particular land base and ecology. For example, in Haudenosaunee country, nations such as the Kanienkeha:ka (Mohawk) utilize the word "skennen" (peace) as part of our normal greeting. "Skennenko:wa ken?"—Is there great peace with you? It is a powerful expression which also serves as a reminder of an important time in Haudenosaunee history where the nations were united in peace after a long period of conflict.

Among Haudenosaunee peoples, we understand that events occurred in the sky world which ultimately led to our existence here. In our origin story, we are told that the first Onkwehonwe, the original people, were told to always greet each other and to greet all of the world around us. We have a ritual called the "Ohenten Karihwatehkwen," that which comes before all other matters. It is a greeting, an acknowledgement, and a thanksgiving which is said before any gathering of people. A speaker is chosen, who it is understood will speak for the gathering. Jake Swamp, a Mohawk faith-keeper who has now passed into the spirit world, often began his address with the words, "We are here to make sure that the cycles of life are continuing." The speaker then acknowledges all the people and may even include the people who are not at the gathering, such as family, clan, and community members, the broader nation, and all other people. The speaker will then say "Teniethinonweraton ne Onkweshon'a," we send our thanksgiving to all the people. "Onen etho neniotonhake ne onkwanikonra," now our minds will be one. At this point, all the people are expected to vocalize their agreement.

The speaker then takes the time to acknowledge all of Creation from the earth to the sky, both seen and unseen, including Mother Earth, the waters, the fish, the medicine plants, the berries, other plants used for foods, the crawling creatures, our four-legged relatives, the birds, the winds, our grandfather thunderers, our elder brother, the Sun, our grandmother Moon, the Stars, the Spirit Beings, and the Creator. After each being, the same phrases are spoken to bring the minds of the people together in greeting and thanksgiving.

The Ohenten Karihwatehkwen is one way to get a glimpse into Haudenosaunee world view. It places people at the centre of a broad web of kinship relationships with other people and with Creation. It is a regular reminder of our ties to one another and to the natural world. The act of engaging in this ritual binds the participants together in a united state of being thankful. It is also a way of building a consensus prior to engaging in any other deliberation. The shared understanding that our existence is inextricably tied to the natural world fulfilling their responsibilities sets out a framework for addressing other matters than may require deliberation.

The Ohenten Karihwatehkwen is one of many rituals and ceremonies which have emerged or re-emerged after a long period of oppression.

Remember that story I told about my grandma and the medicines?

As I grew older, I was fortunate to be able to travel to other First Nations communities, and I had the good fortune to meet with elders and traditional knowledge keepers. I learned that all the medicine plants have names in our language. When we need their assistance, we are to place our words in our sacred tobacco, the one we grow for this purpose, and explain why we need their help. We are only to take what we need. We acknowledge their gift and leave them the tobacco offering. This act of reciprocity reaffirms our understanding of our relationship to the medicine plants, our responsibility to the ones who require the healing and our relationship with all of the natural world. In my community, we no longer had sacred tobacco, yet Grandma still understood the practice of reciprocity and respect when seeking their assistance.

A common experience for most Indigenous peoples is colonization and the forceful suppression of Indigenous languages, cultures, and identities.

In many countries, Indigenous peoples suffered massive population losses from diseases which were previously unknown. Imagine the impact of losing seven, eight, or nine out of every ten people in a community. Imagine the disruption to a family, a community, a nation, and a civilization. When the impact of wars with colonizers or wars inspired by colonialism are added, the decimation of entire nations of Indigenous peoples occurred.

In the early colonial period, many Indigenous nations experienced displacement from our lands. Survival often depended on moving to the most isolated or rugged places imaginable. On other occasions, colonizing authorities forcefully moved Indigenous peoples to such places. Many reserve lands in Canada, federal Crown lands reserved for Indians, were established in rocky outposts, swamplands, or other places which settler populations were likely to find undesirable. Inuit peoples in the northern reaches of Canada were forcibly relocated even further north to enable the Canadian state to enhance territorial claims to the Arctic against competing claims being made by other nations.

Displacement is directly related to economic marginalization. Indigenous communities have been denied adequate services, such as access to clean water, equitable education and health care, and other community infrastructure. As a result, many Indigenous people, including First Nations people, have moved to urban centres. While there are vibrant communities of Indigenous peoples in towns and cities throughout Canada and, indeed, the world, the lasting challenges of living within an entrenched colonial power structure(s) and the pervasiveness of racism continue to be significant barriers to overcome.

The relocation of Indigenous nations to reserves or other types of settlements enabled colonial governments to put measures in place to control

Indigenous peoples. Often traditional forms of social organization and government were replaced with systems of decision-making imposed and/or controlled by colonial authorities. In Canada, Indian agents were appointed to oversee the election of men by men to govern First Nations communities. This had the effect of undermining the traditional leadership role of women and disrupting consensus based decision-making structures. Governments created by colonial authorities were given limited power, working within legislative and budgetary constraints. Over time we have experienced that the new hierarchy created by these structures can be used to fight back against colonial authorities, but they can and have been used to internally oppress their own people.

Education was utilized as a means to destroy Indigenous languages and undermine Indigenous cultural practices. In Canada, residential schools and day schools on reserves would punish students for speaking their language and condemn Indigenous cultures. Some residential schools were engaged in nutritional experiments on Indigenous children.[1] At many schools, students reported being constantly hungry with young women being taught to cook and sew, and young men being taught to work on farms. Many died in residential school[2] or while trying to return home, and many more suffered physical and sexual abuse. Ten members of my own family, including my mom and four of her siblings were sent to three different residential schools throughout Ontario.

The senior bureaucrat in charge of Indian Affairs in the early part of the twentieth century, upon the introduction of a law to require mandatory attendance at residential schools stated:

> *"I want to get rid of the Indian problem. I do not think as a matter of fact, that the country ought to continuously protect a class of people who are able to stand alone….Our object is to continue until there is not a single Indian in Canada that has not been absorbed into the body politic and there is no Indian question, and no Indian department, that is the whole object of this Bill."*[3]

Residential schools did not emerge from thin air. They were designed and supported by government policy to ensure Indigenous peoples would cease to exist as identifiable groups.

MODULE I

The inter-generational impacts on the descendants of the students in residential schools is devastating. Language loss, substance abuse, shame about Indigenous identity, family violence, sexual abuse, social breakdown; these are among the many lasting impacts of generations of education policies and programs designed to enable the disappearance of Indigenous identities from the face of the earth. The former chief justice of the Supreme Court of Canada stated that measures aimed at assimilation amounted to "cultural genocide."[4]

The "Sixties Scoop" where Indigenous children were essentially sold to non-Indigenous parents, primarily in the United States, medical experimentation on Indigenous patients, including forced sterilization of Indigenous women and the ongoing crisis of murdered and missing Indigenous women are among other traumas which have torn at the fabric of Indigenous families and communities, and stem from the legacy of oppressive government policy. The National Inquiry into Missing and Murdered Indigenous Women and Girls issued their final report on June 3, 2019 and noted that:

"The violence the National Inquiry heard amounts to a race-based genocide of Indigenous Peoples, including First Nations, Inuit and Métis, which especially targets women, girls, and 2SLGBTQQIA people. This genocide has been empowered by colonial structures evidenced notably by the Indian Act, the Sixties Scoop, residential schools and breaches of human and Indigenous rights, leading directly to the current increased rates of violence, death, and suicide in Indigenous populations."[5]

The impact on Indigenous identities has been devastating. Indigenous educators Antone, Miller, and Myers identified that "When the cultural beliefs or joyful identity of a people are disrupted" then ethnostress has occurred.[6] The authors note that ethnostress manifests itself in various ways, including an example they call the "hostage syndrome":

"The reservation system acts as a 'captive' environment. During the oppressive years of our existence, outside authorities controlled and dictated various beliefs about ourselves as Indigenous people. Despite recent changes, many of the religious and political beliefs that disrupted our original forms of existence still remain."[7]

Another example is the "narrowing of culture":

"During the course of their historical experience, some Indigenous people lost control of their respective cultures, and consequently, their lives. The 'narrowing of culture' begins with the loss of mobility experienced by the shrinkage of homelands. The cultural experience of Indigenous people became defined by the new, limited environment of the reservation system. The cultural lifestyles were limited by the religious and governmental controls exercised by those who assumed 'authority' over the lives of the people, namely the Indian agents, missionaries, and bureaucrats."[8]

A third example is "culture under glass":

"In this instance, Indigenous culture becomes 'frozen,' as if in a time warp. The concept of 'being Indian' takes on a near exclusive identification with a lifestyle that existed before the loss of mobility (somewhere between 100 to 300 years ago). This idea of Indigenous culture is reinforced by history books that talk about Indigenous people and cultures in the past tense, place anthropological emphasis on what used to be, and denote the recent trend in the courts where the opposition to Native rights argues that changed lifestyle means a particular people no longer exists and, therefore, has no claim to land or other rights."[9]

The authors conclude that ethnostress creates a core problem:

"If an individual accepts a narrow and limited view of culture, the individual has no reason to believe in the culture of his people. Compound this with the idea that the only 'real' Indians existed in another time and space, and you have a person that has very little to grab onto in forming a positive self-image and in imagining a future as an Indigenous person. We end up with a very damaged, insecure, and angry human being, and consequently a very damaged, insecure, and angry community. Individuals and communities who have unfulfilled needs become factionalized by the stress of their very existence, where each faction attempts to fulfill their needs to the exclusion of others."[10]

MODULE I

Despite the carnage, Indigenous peoples have persevered. It is remarkable that Indigenous peoples still exist, despite such a comprehensive colonial assault on our lives and our identities. There are still Haudenosaunee people in this world. There are still Anishinabe. There are still Gitksan and We'tsuet'en and many others. However, just as it took generations of colonialism to create this situation, it is going to take time to restore our positive identities and rebuild our families, clans, communities, and nations.

The validation of our experiences at an individual level, and a collective level is an important part of the learning process and the healing process which needs to occur. In the pages that follow, a number of examples will be introduced to show how the Indigenous portfolio process for the RPL can be utilized to empower individuals and communities based on their lifelong learning experiences.

ENDNOTES

[1] See Mosby, Ian: *Administering Colonial Science: Nutrition Research and Human Biomedical Experimentation in Aboriginal Communities and Residential Schools, 1942-1952*, retrieved from https://hssh.journals.yorku.ca/index.php/hssh/article/download/40239/36424/0

[2] Murray Sinclair, Chair of the Truth and Reconciliation Commission, believes over 6,000 students may have died in residential schools, see https://www.cbc.ca/news/politics/residential-schools-findings-point-to-cultural-genocide-commission-chair-says-1.3093580

[3] Duncan Campbell Scott, 1920, National Archives of Canada, Record Group 10, volume 6810, file 470-2-3, volume 7, pp. 55 (L-3) and 63 (N-3), downloaded from https://tc2.ca/sourcedocs/uploads/images/HD%20Sources%20(text%20thumbs)/Aboriginal%20History/Residential%20Schools/Residential-Schools%2010.pdf, June 5, 2019.

[4] APTN National News: *Canada's top judge says country committed 'cultural genocide' against Indigenous peoples, May 29, 2015*, https://aptnnews.ca/2015/05/29/canadas-top-judge-says-country-committed-cultural-genocide-indigenous-peoples/, retrieved June 2, 2019

[5] National Inquiry into Missing and Murdered Indigenous Women and Girls: Reclaiming Power and Place—The Final Report of the National Inquiry into Missing and Murdered Indigenous Women and Girls, Volume 1a, https://www.mmiwg-ffada.ca/final-report/"https://www.mmiwg-ffada.ca/final-report/, retrieved June 9, 2019, p. 50.

[6]Antone, Robert; Miller, Diane L.; and Myers, Bryan, A.: *The Power Within People—A Community Organizing Perspective*, Peace Tree Technologies, Deseronto, Ontario, 1986, p. 7.

[7]Ibid., p. 16.

[8]Ibid., p. 16.

[9]Ibid., p. 17.

[10]Ibid., p. 17.

Introduction to the First Nations Holistic Learning Model

In 2007 the Canadian Council on Learning facilitated workshops with First Nations, Métis, and Inuit educators to develop culturally relevant holistic learning models as part of a larger project to develop new indicators to measure learning progress for First Nations, Métis, and Inuit learners. The First Nations holistic learning model reflects the learner as integrally connected to their families, clans, ancestors, communities, nations, and to the natural world, and demonstrates there is a link between individual and collective well-being. The individual learner develops intellectually, physically, emotionally, and spiritually, guided by what they learn in formal and informal settings through the course of their lifelong journey. The learning model demonstrates how Indigenous languages, cultures, and traditions contribute to the holistic development of First Nations learners. Indigenous Recognition of Prior Learning (IRPL) is a process by which each of these dimensions of learning can be acknowledged and recognized. In the examples that follow throughout this manual, the reader will be able to recognize how the application of the Indigenous RPL process in each cultural circumstance enables learners to identify their formal and informal learning, and more importantly, develop a realized understanding of their present and an empowered vision of their future.

Introduction to Adult Learning Theory and Practice

This section provides an overview of some important adult learning theory and cultural considerations related to the advisory process and outlines the context, principles, and benefits of portfolio-assisted PLAR.

Initially, key principles of adult learning are discussed in relation to PLAR processes and practices. These guiding principles provide the philosophical

MODULE I

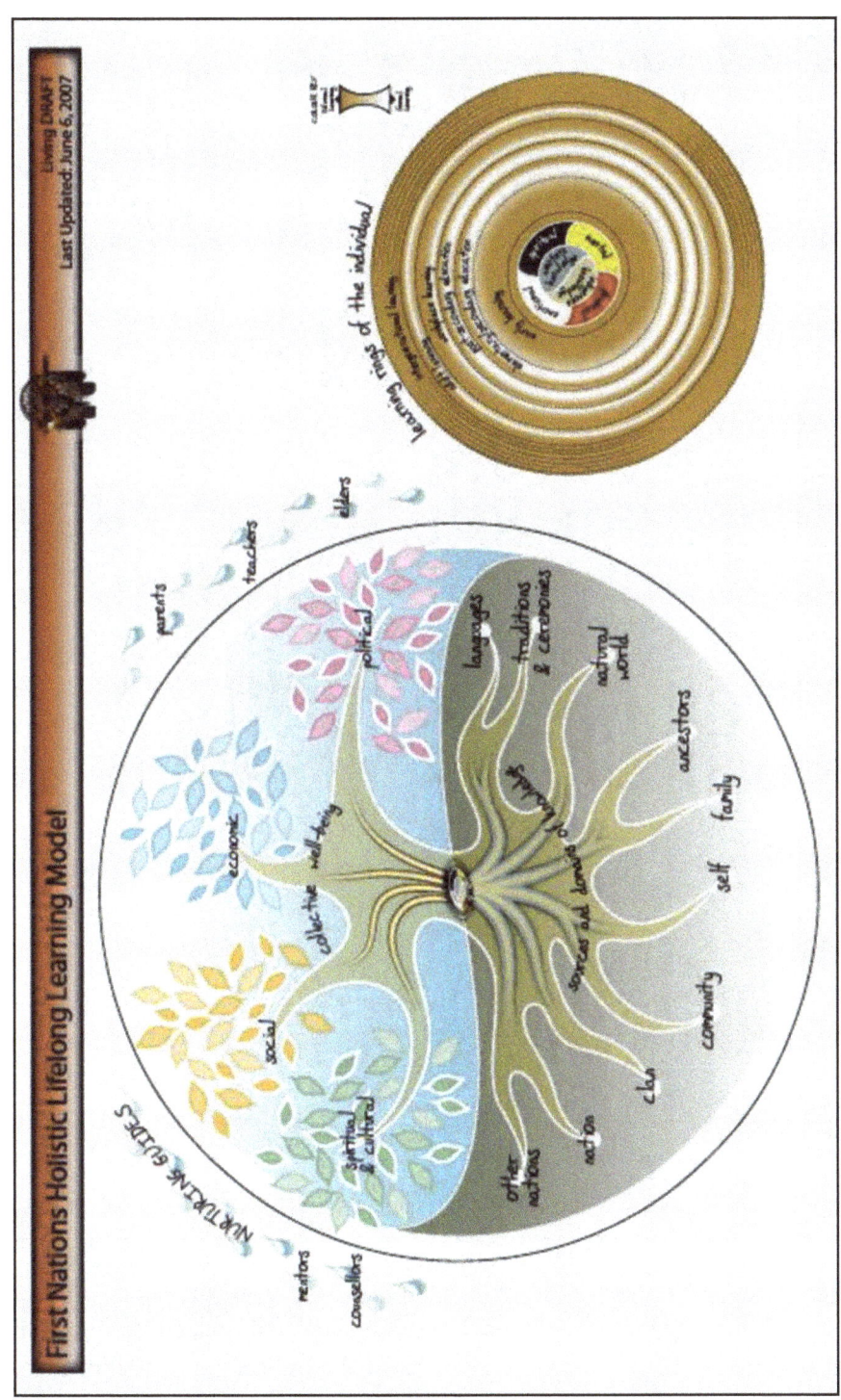

The International Indigenous RPL Practitioner Manual

First Nations Holistic Lifelong Learning Model

Living DRAFT Last Updated: June 6, 2007

ABOUT THE FIRST NATIONS HOLISTIC LIFELONG LEARNING MODEL

The *First Nations Holistic Lifelong Learning Model* represents the link between First Nations lifelong learning and community well-being and can be used as a framework for measuring success in lifelong learning.

For First Nations people, the purpose of learning is to honour and protect the earth and ensure the long term sustainability of life. To illustrate the organic and self regenerative nature of First Nations learning, the Holistic Lifelong Learning Model uses a stylistic graphic of a living tree. The tree depicts the cycles of learning for an individual and identifies the influences that affect individual learning and collective well-being.

The *First Nations Holistic Lifelong Learning Model* is a result of ongoing discussions among First Nations learning professionals, community practitioners, researchers and analysts. For a complete list of individuals and organizations that have contributed to the development of this learning model, visit www.cd-cca.ca.

DESCRIBING THE MODEL

The First Nations learner dwells in a world of continual re-formation, where interactive cycles, rather than disconnected events, occur. In this world, nothing is simply a cause or an effect, but the expression of the interconnectedness of life. These relationships are circular, rather than linear, holistic, and cumulative rather than compartmentalized. The mode of learning for First Nations people reflects and honours this understanding.

Lifelong learning for First Nations peoples is grounded in experiences that embrace both Indigenous and Western knowledge traditions, as depicted in the tree's root system. Sourced and nourishment through its roots, just as the tree draws nourishment through its roots, the First Nations person learns from and through the natural world, language, traditions and ceremonies and the world of people (self, family, ancestors, clan, community, nation and other nations). Any uneven root growth can de-stabilize the learning system. The root system also depicts the intertwining presence of Indigenous and Western knowledge, which forms the tree trunk's core, where learning develops.

A cross-sectional view of the trunk reveals the "Learning Rings of the Individual". At the ring's core are the four dimensions of personal development – spiritual, emotional, physical and metal – through which learning is experienced holistically. The tree's rings portray how learning is a lifelong process that begins at birth and progresses through childhood, youth and adulthood.

Learning opportunities are available in all stages of First Nations life. They can occur in both informal and formal settings such as in the home, on the land or in the school. The stages of learning begin with the early childhood phase and progress through elementary, secondary and post-secondary education, to adult skills training and employment. Intergenerational knowledge is transmitted to the individual form the sources within the roots.

The First Nations learner experiences the various relationships within Indigenous and Western knowledge traditions through their emotional, mental, spiritual and physical dimensions. The tree's extended branches which represent the individual's harmony and well-being, depict the development of these experiences. The individual's well-being supports the cultural, social, political and economic "Collective Well-Being", represented by the four clusters of leaves.

Just as the leaves provide nourishment to the roots and support the tree's foundation, the community's collective well-being rejuvenates the individual's learning cycle. Learning guides – mentors, counselors, parents, teachers and Elders – provide additional support and opportunities for individuals to learn throughout their lifespan.

underpinning for work with adult learners involved in the PLAR process related to helping them meet a variety of personal, cultural, education, and employment goals. The principles will assist the Indigenous practitioner to understand the nature/characteristics of adult learners and offer suggestions about ways to effectively communicate and guide them toward achievement of their goals. The principles identify **the needs of adult learners**, **the role and value of their experiences, their readiness to learn,** and **their orientation to learning**. A central goal is to encourage, support, and empower them to take greater control over their own learning and planning related to personal, cultural, education, training, and employment aspirations.

The application of PLAR and adult learning principles is of benefit in the advisory process. Effective use of adult learning theory and practice within a cultural context can make a significant difference in helping adults to overcome many of the anxieties and fears which they may experience as they contemplate returning to formal study, addressing personal and cultural issues or applying for employment.

The Role of the International Indigenous RPL Practitioner/Advisor

The role of the International Indigenous RPL practitioner is multifaceted. The advisor guides, supports, and nurtures learners as part of the development of a relationship built on mutual trust, respect, and collaboration. Essential components of this evolving relationship include the identification of learner strengths and learning needs. The advisor's role involves many important aspects of the PLAR assessment process. For example, the advisor must be able to help the adult learner identify and document learning related to personal, cultural, education, training, and employment goals and competencies. Advisors help learners to **formatively** (informally) assess their prior learning.

Summative assessment, on the other hand, is the prime responsibility of qualified assessors who determine whether the individual is either competent or not yet competent according to essential competencies. In addition to possessing adult learning skills and knowledge, interviewing and group facilitation skills, advisors must also be skilled in the use of cultural teachings and ceremonies and in assessment theory, portfolio preparation, education, training, and employment requirements and in offering support and encouragement to adults with diverse personal backgrounds, languages, cultures, education, and work histories.

Competencies of the Advisor—The Role of RPL and Adult Learning Principles

ADULT LEARNING THEORY AND PRACTICE

Adult learning principles and cultural teachings form the core of effective practice in the Indigenous RPL process. The Indigenous RPL practitioner is faced with two fundamental questions in most work with adult learners regardless of the circumstances or the setting. They are: what are the essential characteristics of adult learners, and what principles should guide my practice as I attempt to help learners achieve their learning goals?

The development of the field of adult education (theory and practice) has taken place over several decades and has been strongly influenced by a variety of educators from around the world. This includes such noteworthy pioneers as Paulo Friere (Brazil) and Malcolm Knowles (USA). In recent years, others such as Banakonda Kennedy-Kish, Diane Hill, Janice Brant, and Janet Sinclair (Canada) and Kessie Moodley (South Africa) have attempted to adapt adult learning and RPL for application in other cultures and countries by relating RPL principles and practices to the needs of the culture and country. Their work has demonstrated the flexibility of the PLAR process and its tremendous potential to help transform education and training policy and practice internationally.

Malcolm Knowles and Andragogy

Malcolm Knowles began his work on adult learning principles in the 1940s. He developed an approach called "andragogy" which, taken literally, means the art and science of helping adults learn as opposed to teaching them in the traditional (lecture) sense. What Knowles pioneered is a process that actively involves the learner in all aspects of any learning endeavour. He identified four principles around which he built his theory of adult learning.

CONCEPT OF THE LEARNER

One of the first principles articulated by Knowles involves understanding the **concept of the adult learner** as a unique entity. For example, although learners may initially appear to lack confidence in themselves and seem to be dependent on the advisor in the early stages of the relationship, generally they, according to Knowles and others like Friere, have a strong need to be independent. This principle holds that with proper support and encouragement most adults have the ability and potential to become much more capable of making choices about education and training goals that are important to them.

The Indigenous RPL practitioner should work toward supporting and encouraging the learner to move toward greater independence and taking greater control over identifying learning needs and developing plans to achieve them. This does not rule out involving others, such as family and community members, elders, or colleagues in the workplace in the planning process. It means that individuals are expected to take as active a role as possible in charting a learning course for themselves. One of the ways to achieve this goal is by helping learners clarify and state their personal, cultural, education, training, and vocational goals and by providing them with encouragement and support to achieve them. Advisors can encourage learners to take greater control over directing their own learning by helping them recognize and value their own previous learning from a variety of sources.

PREVIOUS LEARNING EXPERIENCES

This principle is related to another important characteristic of adult learners and the significance (power) of their life experiences. Every adult regardless of age, gender, or culture will have had **previous learning experiences**, often of an informal nature, which **serve as a rich resource for future learning** and a foundation for planning. Recognizing and honouring learning from the diverse experiences of adults can be used to enhance self-esteem and self-worth and provide the impetus for them to pursue ongoing learning opportunities. Indigenous RPL practitioners can play a key role by providing initial support and reassurance as adults begin to recognize and value their own experiences, unique gifts, skills, and strengths as learners.

The process of recognizing prior learning for personal and cultural purposes, credit, and recognition regardless of whether the credits are applied in the workplace, in higher education, or at the level of adult basic education and training is sensible and efficient. It does not force adults to repeat learning in areas in which they may be already competent, and it provides them with concrete proof of important learning which they themselves have created from a variety of sources over the course of a lifetime. It helps them value and recognize their own gifts and talents, perhaps for the first time in their lives.

READINESS TO LEARN

The Indigenous RPL practitioner should also acknowledge the adult learner's **readiness to learn** as an essential component of the adult learning process. Adults are generally ready (motivated) to learn when they can see that learning can help them to solve immediate problems, deal with challenges in their lives, or somehow improve their current situation. The Indigenous RPL practitioner must be able to help the learner make (see) the connection between continued learning, personal and cultural goals, their education and career plans, and the benefits that this may bring them. Adults **are practical learners and learn best by doing**, that is, by being active participants in the learning process rather than passive recipients. An important function of the Indigenous RPL practitioner is to ensure that this active involvement takes place within a cultural context.

ORIENTATION TO LEARNING

The Indigenous RPL practitioner must also be aware that the adult learner's **orientation to learning generally will be to strive to become more competent and to achieve greater fulfillment in life**. It seems reasonable to assume that adults generally want to be successful in learning and in their work. The Indigenous RPL practitioner can assist adults by helping them to identify their strengths, gifts, and needs and to minimize the negative impact of any fears or barriers they may encounter as they pursue their learning goals. A supportive, sensitive approach will greatly minimize the chances that the learning experience will be negative or unsuccessful.

Indigenous RPL Practitioner Responsibilities

Your primary responsibility as an Indigenous RPL practitioner is to clear the path for the pursuit of personal, cultural, education, and employment goals by adult learners. You can do this in a number of ways:

MODULE I

- Explore with them what they need to do or know in order to pursue their learning and employment goals.
- Intervene when progress slows and suggest other ways of moving forward.
- Help them see how their skills, knowledge and experience relate to their learning and employment goals and personal, cultural, and educational aspirations.
- Help them identify ways to demonstrate their gifts, skills, knowledge, and attitudes related to these goals/choices.
- React genuinely to their efforts to assess their own skills/knowledge and help them react in a similar fashion.
- Encourage them to find their own answers even when it might be easier for you to supply solutions that seem obvious to you.
- Become a learner with them admitting your own shortcomings—your own need for assistance or additional information.

PLAR and Portfolio-Assisted Assessment

CONTEXT

This section discusses the basic principles, definitions, methods, uses, and strengths of the PLAR process. Particular attention is paid to the basic steps involved in portfolio-assisted PLAR as it applies to learning and employment goals. Indigenous RPL practitioners must be able to competently apply all of the elements of PLAR to help adult learners achieve their learning goals.

PLAR is a valid, reliable educational process through which credentials and qualifications may be achieved in whole or in part through the recognition and validation of prior learning, which includes learning outcomes achieved through formal and informal learning.

PLAR has gradually become a practical, multi-purpose tool for recognizing and assessing the significant learning experiences of adults in a variety of settings, including workplaces and communities. In countries such as Canada, the UK, and South Africa, national standards have been developed to not only ensure the validity and reliability of the PLAR process but also to address specific inequities relating to issues of social justice in a bid to improve access and equity to formal learning opportunities for those who have been poorly served by conventional approaches to education delivery.

This manual focuses on those inequities and injustices as they relate to Indigenous learners and their communities around the world.

PLAR is best viewed as an educational philosophy that promotes democratic values. It can be an important antidote to contemporary forces working against the development of healthy individuals, families, communities, and cultures. It helps adults identify and document their strengths and gifts. It respects individual differences and our inborn ability to solve most of the problems that challenge our survival and ability to function more fully.

Most conventional definitions of PLAR refer, directly or indirectly, to credit, access, learning (formal and informal), assessment, standards, skills, and knowledge. This manual expands that definition to include cultural knowledge, teachings, and ceremonies.

DEFINITION

Prior Learning Assessment and Recognition (PLAR) is a process that involves the identification, documentation, assessment, and recognition of learning acquired through formal and informal study. This may include work and life experience, training, independent study, volunteering, travel, hobbies, family experiences, and cultural teachings. RPL can be used toward the requirements of an academic or training program, occupational/professional certification, or for employment/labour market entry purposes (Canadian Association for Prior Learning Assessment, CAPLA).

PLAR can be used:

- By those seeking admission into further and higher education
- To obtain access into learning programs
- To obtain advanced standing for a course/program
- To obtain credits toward a qualification
- To seek entry into a particular field of employment or professional life
- For registration with professional bodies

MODULE I

- Promotion
- Self development
- For Indigenous knowledge and language development

KEY PURPOSES OF PLAR

- Identifying and strengthening Indigenous knowledge and languages.
- Recognizes the education and training (learning) needs of employers/employees related to important workplace-based skills/knowledge.
- Provides a formal assessment process to demonstrate competency against registered unit standards/qualifications.
- Formally credits learning which demonstrates achievement of specific unit standards/ qualifications/levels.
- Identifies learning gaps and develops specific learning plans to fill them.
- Increases access to important education/training opportunities related to workplace needs.
- Increases access to wider variety of jobs and career path opportunities.
- Facilitates post PLAR plans for specific training/recruitment requirements to meet changing workplace needs.
- Promotes lifelong learning/personal responsibility for need identification and goal setting by unemployed and employed adult learners.

BENEFITS OF PLAR

PLAR can benefit adult learners, faculty, institutions, companies, communities, and cultures.

The benefits to the adult learner are:

1. Eliminates duplication of learning.
2. Streamlines the learning process.
3. Reduces the cost of formal education—take only what you need.
4. Prepares adults to return to formal study:
   a. academically
   b. practically

5. Enhances personal growth/development and self-confidence, strengthening culture, and language.
6. Validates learning from outside the educational system from a variety of sources, including workplaces, communities, and cultural teachings.

The benefits of PLAR to subject matter experts/faculty are:

1. Renewal process—new perspectives on teaching/learning/assessing.
2. Interaction with a more diverse, experienced group of adult learners.
3. Practical, experience-based insights into current applications of the discipline/subject matter.
4. Promotes common assessment principles within academia, in the workplace, and with communities.
5. Broadened understanding of assessment and evaluation.
6. Professional acknowledgement.
7. Opportunity for professional development/new learning experiences.
8. Enriches knowledge of diverse Indigenous cultures and languages.

The benefits of PLAR to institutions/employers are:

1. Recruitment and retention of growing number of diverse, experienced adult learners/workers.
2. Effective tools for placement of learners/ employees and ongoing education/training.
3. Catalyst for organizational self-reflection/change processes.
4. Enhanced access to diverse groups of adults, workplaces, communities.
5. Improved learning environment for all workers/learners—better balance between theory/practice.
6. Good marketing tool—opens up new vistas for educational delivery/on-the-job training, and career path development—more efficient, systematic.
7. Wider range of learning/training options suited to diverse learner/worker needs.
8. Needed service to community, industry, and the larger society.

9. Promotes social justice, respect for a wider variety of Indigenous cultures and languages.

ASSESSMENT METHODS

Candidates seeking formal PLAR recognition/credit must demonstrate attainment of required levels/qualifications/outcomes using a combination of the following assessment methodologies:

- Challenge exams
- Standardized tests
- Demonstration of a particular skill or skill set(s)
- Portfolio-assisted (comprehensive) assessment
- Performance testing
- Structured interviews
- Submission of products, assignments/materials
- Self-assessment and other appropriate types of evidence as determined by the assessor in collaboration with the learner.

ADULT-CENTRED ASSESSMENT METHODS

In helping to prepare adult learners to demonstrate learning related to specific learning/employment goals, it is important for assessors to be as flexible and innovative as possible in the selection of proper assessment tools. For example, for those candidates who may have difficulty with writing, the use of audio-tape recorders may be appropriate to help them document important skills related to specific competencies. This approach is particularly important especially if the competency to be demonstrated does not require the candidate to respond in writing. The use of ***triangulation*** *of evidence* may also be helpful in situations in which a candidate may be able to describe the essential steps of a skill orally instead of in writing, present a piece of his/her own work to demonstrate a finished product, and produce a letter of verification from a supervisor. Assessors should help learners to explore all assessment options/ documentation sources in order to find the best possible method(s) to help them demonstrate learning related to specific competencies. The ultimate goal is to help learners demonstrate their competence confidently and clearly.

Procedures and guidelines specifying the criteria used in the assessment process must be made available to learners, assessors, and advisors well in advance of the assessment itself.

To be considered for recognition/credit through the PLAR process, evidence should meet the following criteria. It must:

- Be appropriate to the learning that is being assessed, including the level and context of the assessment.
- Be verifiable, demonstrated and/or documented.
- Include an appropriate balance of theoretical and practical components consistent with the requirements of the level/qualification being assessed.

Assessment by INDIVIDUAL ASSESSOR or ASSESSMENT PANEL

- Depending upon the nature and complexity of the learning being assessed, assessments may either be done by a panel of assessors or an individual assessor.
- Generally assessment by a single assessor will be the most commonly used approach to assessment.
- Industry accepted tools/methods will be used in performing assessments and recording results.

PLAR and Portfolio Development

PORTFOLIO-ASSISTED PLAR

The portfolio-assisted method of PLAR is particularly well-suited for many adults who are in a state of flux and who need the opportunity and support to conduct a comprehensive personal, educational, or career/occupation self-assessment. This method usually has five basic elements: chronological record, life history, education and career goals, competencies, and documentation. Some PLAR advisors and learners may choose to skip the first two sections and begin the process by defining their education and career goals. For those adults who choose the portfolio-assisted method, it can be a powerful, stabilizing activity. It respects the innate creativity and ingenuity of all human beings, and it acts as a funnel to help adults direct their gifts, talents, and abilities not only to earn formal credit/recognition but to also affirm their worth and enhance their self-esteem.

MODULE I

PLAR AND ADULTS IN TRANSITION

Portfolio-assisted PLAR has much to offer adults who are in transition. It can help them to manage the challenges which accompany change. It provides them with a framework to update their skills and knowledge over their lifetime in a comprehensive, self-directed fashion. It contributes to helping them take stock of their lives, make informed choices about their personal or cultural learning, education, employment goals, and constructively manage the ambiguity which often accompanies change. Adults in transition often need support and guidance to help sort out their situation and to develop and implement plans of action. This is a key aspect of the Indigenous RPL practitioner's role. Changing one's usual ways of thinking and doing takes courage. Setting sail on a somewhat uncharted voyage to an unknown destination is risky and intimidating. Working with adults on the development of portfolios is a privilege. It gives one an intimate, first-hand view of diverse examples of the obstacles which adults regularly overcome in pursuit of their goals, aspirations, and dreams. The portfolio process uncovers individual strengths, assists people to recognize and value their previous learning and their potential in ways that go well beyond the granting of credits or qualifications.

WHAT IS A PORTFOLIO?

The PLAR portfolio is a formal document which identifies learning acquired through a variety of formal and informal learning experiences. It is used to request formal credit/recognition for an individual's learning from experience related to specific learning/employment competencies/goals and qualifications.

Portfolio preparation is an exercise in self-evaluation, introspection, analysis, and synthesis. It is an educational experience in itself. It requires that adults relate their past learning experiences to their personal, cultural, education, and employment goals to exhibit self-analysis, to organize documentation in a clear, concise manner, and relate it to specific competencies related to employment and/or learning goals and qualifications.

Increasingly, portfolios are being used to record the important learning and achievements gained in education and training programs or as heirlooms to pass along to family members. Portfolios, log books, and achievement records are becoming common to those working in a variety of occupations, and it is our belief that they will become more widely used by adults pursuing diverse learning, employment, and cultural opportunities.

WHAT ARE THE CONTENTS OF A PORTFOLIO?

The portfolio is, in many ways, a highly individualized description of the adult's own unique experiences and the learning arising from them. However, there is a certain prescribed format which should be followed, especially if the individual is seeking formal credit/recognition of his/her learning. A portfolio is an effective mechanism for describing and outlining evidence in support of competent performance. It is a practical way for individuals to prove that they are competent in what they do and to identify new personal, educational, and occupational goals.

As a record of one's learning and development over time the portfolio usually includes the following elements:

A Personal Profile—this may take the form of a narrative describing important events in one's life and how they helped to shape the adult learner's current personal, cultural, and occupational situation.

A Goals Paper—describes the adult learner's personal, cultural, occupational, and educational goals.

Evidence of Competence—describes and documents competence related to specific education, training, and employment competencies/levels/qualifications. Areas covered by evidence include documentation drawn from work activities produced by the learner, evidence from others about the adult learner's skills and abilities, a description of their current occupational situation and the context in which he/she is working.

A major outcome of the portfolio development process is that it has the potential to be a powerful statement about the individual's skills and competence related to specific learning and employment skills, knowledge, and attitudes. The portfolio should be constructed within a clearly defined, systematic framework, be supported by reference to documentation sources, be able to verify the candidate's skills/competence, describe the context in which the candidate has been learning/working, be easy to

MODULE I

read and understand, and make allowance for the individual's own unique personal style and life/work history.

As a result of participating in the portfolio development process, adult learners should be able to:

- Describe the conditions under which one should participate in the portfolio development process, the basic elements of a portfolio, and the role of the advisor;
- Review existing competence (self-assessment) related to specific learning/employment competencies and identify appropriate sources of evidence to demonstrate competence;
- Recognize the value and legitimacy of learning from experience and that learning is a lifelong, ongoing process;
- Assemble a portfolio of evidence for credit/recognition related to specific cultural or learning/employment competencies;
- Develop a learning plan for achieving cultural, personal/occupational, or educational goals.

WHAT ARE THE STEPS IN THE PORTFOLIO DEVELOPMENT/EVALUATION PROCESS?

With the help of the Indigenous RPL practitioner, individuals will work through the following steps in the portfolio development process. They will:

- Reflect on their prior experiences and examine what they have learned related to specific education, cultural or occupational goals.
- Clarify their cultural, educational, occupational, and personal objectives in the light of past learning experiences and develop an education/career plan. With the assistance of the Indigenous RPL practitioner, identify and record learning they have acquired from a variety of sources and relate it to specific education/ occupational/cultural competencies to demonstrate equivalency.
- Prepare suitable evidence to document the learning for which they are seeking credit and/or recognition.
- Complete the portfolio, which includes a personal profile/narrative, a statement of cultural, educational, career and personal

objectives, a clarification of experiences and related learning, and supportive documentation. The portfolio will demonstrate how the learning is related to particular competencies or outcomes related to specific education/occupation goals. Their specific request for credit/ recognition related to the identified learning is also included.
- Submit their portfolio for informal evaluation by the Indigenous RPL practitioner (advisor) who will return it to them with specific comments for revisions or corrections as warranted.
- Submit their portfolio for formal evaluation by a qualified assessor or team of assessors based on the type of credit/recognition requested.
- Have any formal credit/recognition which is awarded, recorded in their file/transcript in the manner in which competencies/outcomes related to specific educational/ occupational achievements are usually recorded.

ADDITIONAL BENEFITS OF COMPILING A PORTFOLIO

As a record of one's achievements, including one's growth and development, personally, culturally, and occupationally, a portfolio can have long-term, lasting benefits. As individuals begin the process of compiling a portfolio, they should be able to

- Recognize their own skills/competencies and how they can be further developed. The process should help them identify their strengths and gaps in learning.
- Reflect upon their day-to-day activities at work, home, and in the community. This should encourage them to become more thoughtful and focused in their overall approach in each of these spheres.
- Demonstrate greater self-confidence and enhanced motivation to pursue learning activities which will help them meet cultural, personal, educational, and work-related needs/goals.

Adults who have completed portfolios often find that they can reflect upon and evaluate the performance of others as well as their own performance. As a result of this increased sensitivity and self-confidence they are able to recognize competence more accurately and quickly in others and to acknowledge it positively.

MODULE II

The Role of RPL in Addressing Issues of Social Justice, Inequality, Oppression, and Educational Reform

Introduction

This module describes the role of RPL and portfolio development in addressing long-standing issues related to social justice, inequality, oppression, and educational reform in Canada, South Africa, and Chile. In each example, the approach taken to RPL implementation varies from country to country in part because oppression, inequality, and racism exist in many different forms and structures. The flexibility and adaptability of RPL and portfolio development is highlighted in this module as is the determined, ongoing commitment to social change by Indigenous peoples and their allies in the three countries.

Module Outcomes

Upon successful completion of this module, participants should be able to:

- Discuss the variety of ways in which RPL and portfolio development have been implemented in Canada, South Africa, and Chile.
- Describe the role of RPL and portfolio development in addressing issues of social justice, inequality, oppression, and educational reform in the three countries.
- List three examples of ways that RPL and portfolio development might be implemented in their home communities.

CANADA

Strengthening Indigenous Cultures and Languages, Promoting Healing and Social Justice in Canada

The Truth and Reconciliation Commission of Canada released its report in 2015 with a number of calls to action. It is a critical event in the long history of the relationship between Canada and Indigenous peoples in Canada. The challenges set in motion by the process of reconciliation have caused many organizations and institutions to review their existing mandates and daily functions. Many have realized that implementation of the report's calls to action are not as straightforward or as clear-cut as it may have appeared to be in the beginning. Instead it has turned out to be a rather complex process with many twists and turns.

Post-secondary institutions are key partners in the change process across Canada, and many have implemented strategies aimed at making their organizations more respectful of Indigenous teachings and ways of knowing and ensuring that Indigenous beliefs and values are reflected in the day-to-day operations of their institutions and that communities are being consulted as true partners in the process.

One example of an institution that is actively involved in the change process is Vancouver Island University (VIU) in Nanaimo, British Columbia. What follows is a document that was created with input from the Elders in Residence at VIU providing local context in relation to truth and reconciliation and the work of decolonization.

Conversations Toward Reconciliation and Healing

We would like to acknowledge that the main campus of VIU is on the territories of the Snuneymuxw peoples. We recognize and appreciate the opportunities and privileges of learning and working together on their lands.

MODULE II

The Wisdom of the Old People...

Through stories, our old people provide rich glimpses into the past that help to broaden and develop the minds of those who know how to listen. Our elders speak of times when our communities numbered in the thousands as we gathered and respectfully feasted on the rich life energies found within our territories. Our old people speak of the importance of having and demonstrating respect for everything around us, and our place within the delicate cycles of the cosmos. They also share a guiding vision about the importance of holding each other up and making sure everyone is cared for, especially during the toughest of times. Holding each other up is the responsibility we all have to add to the fire that burns in others in a good way. In addition, our elders remind us about the stories that tell us we have been here for thousands of years and of the importance of retelling these stories to Indigenous peoples to ensure our continued connection to the land, culture, and ceremonies. These old stories tell us of the arrival of Europeans long before their boats reached our shores and the devastation that followed. Moreover, the old people stress the importance of remembering that our stories as Indigenous peoples do not begin with colonization, and of the consequences of placing this dark history at the centre of our lived experiences in contemporary times. Finally, it is through our stories that we get intimate glimpses of the beauty, resilience, and strength of the world in which our ancestors lived, which help to guide and support us today. In italicized sections scattered throughout this document, our elders share their wisdom and knowledge of our histories in their own words.

Where We Come From

Coast Salish people acknowledge that learning is grounded in who we are and where we are from. We believe this to be true for all of us. With this in mind, it is important to ensure our conversations include the following:

- Why and how we acknowledge our unceded territories
- The significance of place and identity

Harold Joe sheds light on the importance of respecting his territory:

"There's nothing but gratitude for Mother Earth. When you walk in the woods, you get in harmony with the trees because they are the ones that give you shelter. You walk in harmony with the animals; they also feed you. They sacrifice their lives. That's why there is so much gratitude for Mother Earth. I'm in harmony with Mother Earth because I'm still walking out here." Yut'xwam—Harold Joe, VIU Elder

In a related vein, Uncle Gary speaks about how his great-great-grandfather's relationship to the land contributes to his own identity:

"What was taken away lives spiritually, but not in my memory. I can almost picture my great-great-grandfather with a cedar cape sitting on a canoe somewhere after cold water bathing. Not for a spiritual sense, but to make his body strong in order to endure the north wind or the southwesterly wind." Xulsimalt—Gary Manson, VIU Elder

Foundational

It is important to note that the term *Aboriginal* is a colonially sanctioned construct that has limitations in regards to the identity and inherent rights of Indigenous peoples. The descendants of the peoples who inhabited these lands long before the colonial invasion of 1492, on the other hand, may use the term *Indigenous*, which does not carry the same restrictions as the colonially sanctioned term *Aboriginal*. In addition, by using *Indigenous*, these people link themselves to the liberation efforts of more than 370 million self-identified Indigenous people worldwide who are confronting historic and ongoing colonization.

The Canadian constitution recognizes three groups within the definition of *Aboriginal*:

MODULE II

- First Nations
- Métis
- Inuit

They are distinct peoples with unique histories, languages, cultural practices, and spiritual beliefs. According to the 2006 Census, more than one million people in Canada identify as Aboriginal.

Aboriginal communities are located in urban, rural, and remote locations across Canada. VIU main campus is located on the unceded territory of the Coast Salish peoples, including Snuneymuxw (Nanaimo), Stz'uminus (Chemainus) and Snaw-Naw-As (Nanoose First Nation). Other regional campuses are located on Cowichan Tribes and Tla'Amin First Nation territories. In addition, the Mid Island Métis Nation has an office to serve its members and the Tillicum Lelum Aboriginal Friendship Centre offers a wide range of services to all Aboriginal groups, on reserve or off-reserve.

A central component of *reconciliation* is the concept of *decolonization*. These two terms are complex and can mean different things to different people depending on numerous external and internal influences and expectations.

Decolonization: To provide some perspective, Snuneymuxw and VIU Elder Geraldine Manson talks about decolonization practices within the classroom:

> *"Decolonization is to take a moment and the time to understand your Indigenous students. Understand where your student is coming from when they come into your class. Understand that the student comes into your class full of wisdom. They are coming to learn what you have within yourself, but you need to understand that that student's wisdom is equal to yours. So, if you take the time to understand the individual as the individual is coming to understand what you share, then both of you have walked down that path together with respect. That's decolonizing your mind. Respect what the individual has and recognize you're no better just because you're the instructor. As the instructor, you are there to learn from them." C-tasi:a—Geraldine Manson, VIU Elder*

Similarly, we recognize that the perspectives we share are not the only truths to be considered, but rather form a small part of a much larger understanding that we are building together. Related to this idea, Aunty Geraldine reminds us of the importance of reconciliation:

> "Reconciliation is a word that breeds respect. If we were to understand how our ancestors lived, we would see they were always taking care of one another: from the morning when they got up to the evening when they went to bed. Everything was taken care of. Reconciliation included the young and the old. For those who were ill to those who had passed, all the needs were taken care of. From the water to the land to the environment…from the mountains to the rivers to the ocean to the whole environment, there needs to be reconciliation. No one is better than anyone else. We must listen to everyone's voice. From the homeless to the old, everyone's voice must be included in understanding reconciliation. That's what it means to me." C-tasi:a—Geraldine Manson, VIU Elder

Aunty Geraldine's words suggest that meaningful reconciliation extends beyond the boundaries of human relationships. From her perspective, we have a responsibility to reconcile with the animals, lands, water, and plant life in a way that sees them equal to human beings. However, again, we must stress that the terms *decolonization* and *reconciliation* mean different things to different people.

Reconciliation: Snuneymuxw and VIU Elder Gary Manson shares what he is doing to achieve a sense of reconciliation in his own life:

> "For me, reconciliation is the honouring of myself. To be good human beings with each other and not letting the wounds of our pride get in the way of this. It is not so much reconciling with the settlers, but with each other and sharing that. That's the healing that needs to take place. For me, we need to get ourselves together. For me right now, I can only do it within my own house. If I do it in my own house, I will set an example. It's okay to be afraid but do what you need to do. Sing that song. Dance that song. Surround yourself with the people you need and, 'Don't be ashamed.' Those were my uncle's favourite words." Xulsimalt—Gary Manson, VIU Elder

MODULE II

History of Truth and Reconciliation Commissions

Globally, the truth and reconciliation process has a short history, with the first TRC held in Argentina in 1983. Depending on the location and matters being addressed, these commissions have been named differently. For example, National Commission, Truth Commission, Reconciliation and Unity Commission, Historical Clarification Commission, and Lessons Learned and Reconciliation Commission, to name but a few. No matter what name is chosen, the TRC process is a tool for investigating and, hopefully, resolving human rights violations resulting from state and non-state approved terrorism against marginalized groups of people. These serious human rights violations include land theft, assassination, murder, torture, rape, kidnapping, imprisonment, and the disappearance of marginalized members, but abuse is not limited to these practices alone. In short, the TRC process is used in places where genocide has occurred in the hope that relations between parties can somehow be repaired. Some people prefer to use *cultural genocide* when discussing Canada's colonial history, but an argument for simply using *genocide*, as defined by the United Nations, can be made quite easily when looking at the historic and contemporary relationships between the Canadian state and the Indigenous peoples of these lands. The mandates of TRCs are usually quite narrow but vary depending on the matters under investigation. While many people see benefits to the TRC process—truth telling practices, recording of history, research, and finding ways to overcome past abuse—others are critical. What many critics find problematic is how those identified as abusers and guilty of human rights violations may go unpunished—and in fact, may even be protected from prosecution under TRC processes—but this is not always the case.

While all thirty-one TRCs are important for how they have addressed the loss of human life on a massive scale, we have chosen only a few as examples to reveal the seriousness of this conversation. The first TRC was established in 1983 in Argentina to investigate the disappearance of 30,000 people during a time of political turmoil. Death squads were thought to have been responsible for many of the killings. It was the first time since the infamous Nuremburg trials prosecuted Nazi war criminals that a civilian court held trial for war crimes. Another notable TRC example is Chile's National Commission for Truth and Reconciliation, which addressed the unjustified political imprisonment and torture of approximately 38,000 people and the murder of a lesser number from 1973–90. Finally, one of the better-known TRCs emerged in South Africa in response to tensions between Indigenous South Africans and Dutch colonizers. This TRC drew international attention with the release of Nelson Mandela in 1990 after twenty-seven years of unjustified imprisonment. The reason for the TRC was that the Dutch colonial state had forcibly removed Indigenous South Africans from their homelands and made them live in racially segregated neighbourhoods. Dismantling the ideas and systems supporting racial segregation ideas and practices in South Africa proved to be a difficult task. In fact, the anti-apartheid movement was met with resistance and violence as the Dutch colonial powers were determined to hold on to their rule of Indigenous lands, resources, and peoples that were not theirs to control.

Canada and the TRC

In Canada, the TRC process faces some of the same challenges already mentioned when it comes to addressing land theft, racial segregation, legislated kidnapping of Indigenous children, and murders of Indigenous leaders committed to resisting colonization, dismantling the ideas and systems that support further crimes against humanity, and entering into a relationship that sees the state relinquishing its iron grip on Indigenous lands, resources, and identities, to name but a few. In Canada, the TRC conversation commenced in 2008 and completed its mandate in 2015. However, this conversation has been limited to discussing only residential schools and the human rights violations stemming from this government and church-sponsored project, while seemingly ignoring other historical and ongoing genocidal ideologies and practices against Indigenous peoples and their homelands. Moreover, since the residential school crimes against Indigenous people did not happen during the colonial criteria of what constitutes "a time of war," state actors identified as being abusers (including the church, provincial and federal government representatives, the police force, the military, and corporate leaders) cannot be prosecuted for war crimes, which is disturbing and needs to be questioned. *Why do some people seem to escape accountability and punishment for participating in historical and ongoing crimes against humanity when others cannot? Can the criteria be changed to address the reality that crimes against humanity do happen outside of times of war?* These are examples of some of the more challenging questions we have to ask ourselves when we open our minds to what meaningful reconciliation looks like among the peoples who inhabit the colonial landscape of Canada.

Related to these challenging questions, Aunty Marlene shares her thoughts on the seriousness of the work that still needs to be done with Canadians:

> "*Reconciliation with the government will never happen until Canadians accept in their hearts what happened to the Indigenous peoples. How can the settlers understand or know what we need when they do not know what we are about? Until they face that fact, then this truth and reconciliation is not going to work. Acceptance and accountability have to be part of this new foundation if we are to move forward. When people are held accountable for their actions, then we can begin looking at a really true healing process for people. Finding our old ways, our own teachings in our homeland, and not sending our people off somewhere.*" Hwiem'—Marlene Rice, VIU Elder

Copyright © http://www.viu.ca/, Vancouver Island University
Produced by http://www.viu.ca/aboriginal, Office of Aboriginal Education

PLAR and portfolio development is being used to support the documentation and affirmation of Indigenous knowledge and as a tool to counteract the negative impact of colonization in its many forms. "The portfolio has been successfully utilized to assist Indigenous learners to reframe or reassess their experiences as Indigenous peoples. It has also been used to identify, document, and validate the skills, ceremonies, and practices of Indigenous peoples in Canada often leading to a path of healing, and as a result, a greater ability to improve one's life and develop the capacity to reciprocate this to others. Translating traditional ways of knowing, protocols, rituals, ceremonies and language into beliefs, values sets, and skill sets illustrates the power of the portfolio to recognize how, for example, land-based, traditional Indigenous knowledge is relevant today. In this important time of truth and reconciliation in Canada, we have been able to access the power of PLAR and the portfolio to comprehend the truth about the hardships posed by colonization and the appropriation of Indigenous peoples of their lands, languages, seeds, their images, designs, clothing, technologies, tools, and stories" (Janice Brant, 30th Annual PLAR Conference).

There are detailed examples in module IV of three culturally based Indigenous portfolios arising from Indigenous practice using portfolio development in their respective communities. The examples are the Coast Salish in British Columbia, the Haudenosaunee in Ontario, and the Inuit in Nunavut.

SOUTH AFRICA

Using the Recognition of Prior Learning (RPL) as a Tool for Social Action in South Africa

[This is written about RPL at the Workers' College up until January 2016 when I retired. I cannot attest as to whether such approach and practices still prevail at the College.] (Kessie Moodley)

In 1992, the Workers' College was established. It was a time when South Africa was undergoing radical political change. The abhorrent policy of apartheid, the White colonial policy of racial discrimination, came to an end and the Black majority in the country were given political rights. However, the racially skewed capitalist economic policy still prevailed which ensured that the wealth remained in the hands of the White minority and in the hands of national and global corporations. The Black majority were still being economically exploited, socially excluded, and remained in deprived conditions of existence. In the education sphere, while access to education, at all levels, was being opened to those who were denied, excluded and deprived from it previously, the content and delivery of such education still ensured that a colonial, elitist, and market-driven mindset prevailed.

The Workers' College developed into an **alternate 'education' organization**, seeing itself more as bringing about change rather than endorsing the dominant, mainstream educational approach. It identified with a particular broader civil society constituency and embraced education as a means of collective consciousness and activism. Trade union and community activists were the participants in the governance and programs of the college and, through the programs, sought to strengthen their capacities and insights to strengthen their representation of workers and communities from whence they hailed.

The preamble to the Workers' College's Constitution captures its location as an education organization:

> *"We, the participating trade union federations, trade unions and civic organizations, who constitute the Workers' College Council, hereby declare our commitment to the working class struggle to build egalitarian values and horizontal participatory and democratic traditions and processes in education and in the broader socio-political arena.*
>
> *"The dominant education discourse and practices serve to entrench social stratification and maintain the capitalist class structure that is driven by greed, individualism, crass materialism and the commodification of life."*

Approach to Education Practice

The Workers' College must be seen as a platform, a site, an organization, and a resource that developed and strengthened forms of activism through education. To this end the following elements, values, and approaches were adopted and practised:

- Development of a culture of commitment to struggle for change and a sense of volunteerism for collective action;
- Collectivism that encouraged a departure from selfishness and individualism and inculcated a sense of togetherness and common good;

- Humaneness, love, respect, compassion as essential, core values;
- Self-reliance to determine one's own destiny;
- Critical and objective thinking for effective development;
- Freedom of expression;
- Self-reflection and a continuous learning process;
- Solidarity and accompaniment by staff, facilitators, and participants to support each other on the education journey;
- Accountability and transparency to ensure collective ownership, trust, sustainability, and responsibility;
- Response to challenges in a practical way;
- Creation of a platform where participants, facilitators, and staff are exposed to new, constructive knowledge and learning practices;
- Utilization of the resources of the college for the benefit of the collective, of the broader society, of the greater good—this applied to staff, facilitators, participants, as well as individuals and organizations that interacted with the college.

The college's approach to education was that the method of engagement with the educational content was connecting the experiential learning and knowledge of the participants, all of whom were activists, with theoretical and academic knowledge. This pedagogy was steeped in an adult education approach with a specific focus on equipping trade union and community activists with practical and theoretical capacities to strengthen their activism and their organizational practice. This approach is shaped by the history of Workers' College as a worker-centred, civil, society-based organization born from the liberation struggle and grappling with the complexities and intricacies of a neo-liberal, democratic dispensation in a globalized world.

The Recognition of Prior Learning (RPL)

While drawing on the experiences of adult participants was always central to the education practice at the Workers' College since its inception in 1992, this process was never formalized, or rather, it was never given any name! The formal and conscious introduction of the Recognition of Prior Learning (RPL) took place after the then Joint

MODULE II

Education Trust (JET), a South African non-profit education organization, in 2005 conducted a research project into the alternative access route of the Workers' College's diploma program. On completion of the research and discussions around its findings, JET invited the Workers' College to attend a PLAR/RPL conference held by First Nations Technical Institute (FNTI). Subsequent to the conference the college participated in a study tour of Canada and North America around the issue of PLAR/RPL. This visit inspired and stimulated the Workers' College to look holistically at RPL as a method of bringing about personal and organizational transformation.

FNTI had also implemented a set of guidelines for education institutions and community-based organizations to cater to the needs of their adult students. These 'tools' are referred to as the **Adult Learner Friendly Institute (ALFI) principles**, a set of benchmark principles that serve as statements of best practice and against which the Workers' College could assess itself. It was clear that these principles created an institutional context conducive to RPL, and that they spoke directly to an approach that integrated RPL into the college's overall ethos and practices. The Workers' College adopted these principles, with some contextual amendments, as a set of tools to be applied to its organizational form as an educational organization.

At the time of political transition in South Africa in the early 1990s, the RPL was being introduced into the national education and training policy discourse as a means of effecting transformation, and of addressing issues of access, articulation, and equity. RPL usually took, and continues to take, the form of an assessment tool which takes place before entry into a program of learning.

RPL was seen as an educational practice at the Workers' College that facilitated the validation of all learning experienced by individuals and groups of individuals or communities. The approach was based on the premise that all teaching and learning events should be designed to begin with the participants' experiences and build from this point. The Workers' College educational philosophy was to begin with the participants' struggle knowledge, to reflect on it and validate it through peer engagement, and to link such experiential knowledge to the theoretical, codified knowledge base of the academy.

The International Indigenous RPL Practitioner Manual

The fight against colonial rule, political oppression, economic exploitation, social exclusion, and apartheid subjected to by the majority of the people of South Africa, predominantly Black people (this included the majority African population as well as people who were classified "Coloured" and those who were classified "Indian"), was referred to as the **struggle.** This term was, and still is, used to reflect the fight against apartheid as it captured how long this oppression was imposed, how hard it was fought, and the kind of commitment needed to engage in this battle. It also refers to the fight for a just, egalitarian society, which seeks to address the social, economic, political, and cultural imbalances of the global and national system of oppression and exploitation of the majority of people by an elite minority.

Arising from these circumstances the concept of **struggle knowledge** developed. This is a body of knowledge that was acquired through lived experiences in fighting for one's rights, your dignity, your survival, against terrible forms of oppression, violence, exploitation and being subjected to inhumane forms of treatment and indignity. It is through this lived experience that people developed ways in which to survive, to raise their families, to build communities, to develop values and practices of waging struggle, to create organizations to mobilize against oppression and exploitation, all this achieved both individually and collectively.

RPL was thus woven into the development of the program and materials, the teaching, facilitating, and learning practice, and to some extent, the assessment.

The potential of RPL was that it provided the college with the possibility to create an environment and learning space that allowed its participants and facilitators to:

- Find their own voice and self-respect, given that they were coming from realities that denied them their basic dignity.
- Inculcate a sense of confidence and pride in themselves and their heritage as well as a sense of collectivism.
- Critically reflect on their strengths and examine their weaknesses.
- Develop a sense of individual and collective history.
- Engage critically with conventional knowledge and determine its relevance.

MODULE II

- Find alternative solutions to the challenges facing them within their workplaces, communities and organizations that drew on their own experiences, both individual and collective, and that spoke to the greater good for the collective.
- Discover that the power to change rested with themselves, both as individuals and as a collective.
- Identify with values and principles that informed their world view, the way they saw themselves, and how they treated their comrades.
- See themselves as activists.

The core educational programs of the Workers' College were four (4) diploma courses, namely, labour studies, gender and labour studies, labour economics, and political and social development studies. While each diploma course was comprised of six modules, there were two modules that were common to all four diplomas, namely, activism and field work.

Field Work was a module that was facilitated throughout the year of study and had as its main aim the exposure of participants to the realities of the society at large. This was the opportunity for the participants to apply their experience, knowledge, and acquired learnings and insights in the communities from whence they came and in the constituencies that needed change. The module challenged them to work with and amongst vulnerable workers, for example, during their period of study. This exposure gave them a first-hand experience of what others were facing, shared with them their hardships and challenges, and they then were expected to apply their own experiences as to how some of those challenges could be overcome.

Activism as the Foundational Module

Activism was developed as a foundational module that introduced all participants to the concept and approach of RPL. Its main aim was to develop and reinforce a basic consciousness and understanding of values and practices of activism through RPL.

The objectives of the module were to:

- Raise participants' awareness of their own values and activism practices;
- Recognize and validate participants' knowledge, experiences, and practices as activists and potential activists;
- Engage with the various forms, methods, and sites of activism;
- Explore and understand practices that negate activism and develop strategies to address and prevent them from recurring;
- Become aware that part of education was bringing about change through activism.

The module was conducted over a week in ten, two-hour residential sessions. Facilitators of the sessions were all drawn from activist backgrounds so that their own experiences and learnings were shared with those of the participants. There was no hierarchy but rather horizontal participation. Participants and facilitators saw themselves as part of a common journey in strengthening activism to bring about social change. The sessions were designed with specific outcomes and a range of interactive activities and audio-visual aids, centred around the participant, and used to facilitate the sessions.

The following topics were facilitated in the activism module, with their outcomes and activities listed:

- Activism and values
- Forms and methods of activism
- Sites of activism and realities of struggle
- Practices that negate activism
- Activism and power
- Assignment

MODULE II

ACTIVISM AND VALUES

Outcomes: at the end of these sessions, participants should be able to do the following:

- Identify values that inform their own activism, practice, and locate their experience within the broader economic, socio- political, and cultural contexts.
- Explain the concepts, *activism* and *values* and the relationship between them.

Facilitated Activities:

Individual exercise: write one (1) page about themselves as a family member, as a community member, and as an activist.

Group exercise: share and discuss in groups the values that participants considered non-negotiable; discuss how they as individuals and as a group, applied these values in relation to race, gender, and class in their families, organizations, workplaces, and communities. Each group is to capture on a flipchart the values they considered non-negotiable and to provide an example of how they would apply one of these values in their homes, organizations, workplaces, and communities.

Individual exercise: "An Island has been discovered recently and twelve (12) people need to be selected to go and live there for fifty (50) years and create a new society." Individually, participants were asked to select the twelve people from a list that included people from various racial, class, gender, age, unskilled, skilled, foreign, disabled, status, political, social and activist backgrounds, and they had to state the reason for selecting those they chose and the reason for rejecting the remaining people.

Plenary exercise: each participant to argue why they made their selection and for the plenary to arrive at a common list.

FORMS AND METHODS OF ACTIVISM

Outcomes: at the end of these sessions, participants should be able to do the following:

- Explain various forms and methods of activism.
- Describe the relationship between the forms and methods of activism.

- Contextualize the various forms and methods of activism within the South African situation.

Facilitated Activities:

All participants participated in a role play. The scenario created was that as a member of a community that was described, they had to collectively discuss an intervention or action that they would take in response to a problem bedevilling the community. The problem was that the community was living in an informal settlement which had no proper facilities to service the community, such as roads, clean water, electricity, and proper public transport. There were also a lack of social services, such as no clinics, proper schools, and parks. These realities led to people living in squalid conditions and led to the increase in social evils, such as crime, drug taking, and gangsterism.

The participants had to prepare the role play that depicted the various interest groups in the community, how they would normally respond or behave, and then how the group would introduce an intervention or action that would try to resolve the problem.

The interest groups that were identified included the following:

- Taxi operators and informal traders
- Landlords, rich homeowners, and business people
- Gender activists, environmentalists, and health workers
- Sex workers, tavern owners, and gangsters
- Trade unionists and student organizations

SITES OF ACTIVISM AND REALITIES OF STRUGGLE

Outcomes: at the end of these sessions, participants should be able to:

- Identify what are sites of activism and realities of struggle and their relevance to activism.
- Develop an approach that includes understanding the opportunities and weaknesses that such sites present for activism and develop strategies and tactics in tackling the realities.

Facilitated Activities:

A discussion ensues, with input from the facilitator, as to what a site of activism is and what are realities of struggle.

MODULE II

Thereafter, participants, in pairs, determine how many other sites of activism and realities of struggle they can identify, with reasons as to why they have been so identified. These are listed individually and shared with the group, and a discussion ensues as to whether there is agreement on the suggested sites of activism and realities of struggle.

Facilitator's Input:

Activism is a concerted effort aimed at either challenging, transforming, reforming, or preserving the prevailing material conditions (socio-political, economic, and cultural realities, systems, structures, and values). This can be done through individual and/or collective action and advocacy using a wide range of methods and platforms. The choice of methods and platforms depend on the form of activism, the values, and world view (ideology) that informs the activism, the site in which the activism occurs, and the socio-political, economic, and cultural realities within a particular place and era.

Site of activism is a place which provides the possibility of advancing our beliefs and values. It is a place or a space which is a physical environment, such as home, the community, workplace, organization, taxi, queue, shopping mall, street, market, meeting, government offices. Wherever we find ourselves in the company of others, there is the possibility of sharing our ideas and values. Of course, the fundamental approach to any activism that takes place is for everyone to be heard, for everyone to participate, and to be directly involved in shaping whatever action or decision that is to be taken.

PRACTICES THAT NEGATE ACTIVISM

Outcomes: at the end of these sessions, participants should be able to:

- Critique their own activism practices and that of their organizations.
- Determine the basis for such negative practices to exist.
- Explore ways to overcome such negative practices.

Facilitated Activities:

Plenary—Input from facilitator: "The struggle against homophobia, xenophobia, and gender inequality is an integral aspect of the struggle to overcome racism, sexism, and class oppression in our organizations and society broadly. The struggle to overcome racism, sexism, and class oppression will be incomplete if it does not address other related forms of social discrimination and oppression. Therefore, it is important to address and combat all these forms of oppression in our struggle to create a free and equal society." Discussion ensues as to whether such practices still prevail, why, and possibilities as to how to overcome them.

In pairs, participants study the cartoon below and explain:

- What message it seeks to convey?
- How it is related to the session topic?
- List three other examples of practices that negate values of activism?
- Capture their responses on the cards given to them.

ACTIVISM AND POWER

Outcomes: at the end of these sessions, participants should be able to:

- Analyze how power is distributed, exercised, and expressed in different social settings.
- Explain how power shapes and influences activism.
- Explore forms of distribution, exercise, and expression of power that promotes activism and the values of democratic participation, equality, justice, and respect of the dignity of all people.

MODULE II

Facilitated Activities:

In groups participants read the article below and discuss how the expressions of power listed and explained in the article operate and manifest themselves in (1) their homes, (2) their communities, (3) their organizations, and (4) their workplaces. In examining how power is expressed at these sites, they consider the following:

- Who gets listened to best?
- Who takes up most time talking?
- Who does not get heard?
- If someone says nothing, do people notice?
- What types of privileges and rewards are there, and who gets most of the privileges and rewards?

ARTICLE ON POWER

Expressions of Power

Power is often defined only in negative terms and as a form of domination, but it can also be a positive force for individual and collective capacity to act for change. Lisa VeneKlasen and Valeries Miller in *A New Weave of Power* (2002, page 55) describe four expressions of power as follows:

Power Over

[Cartoon: Two people seated in chairs. One says: "We're most happy to fund your HIV programs. AS LONG AS they don't promote condom use..."]

The most commonly recognized form of power, **power over**, has many negative associations for people, such as repression, force, coercion, discrimination, corruption, and abuse.

Power is seen as a win-lose kind of relationship. Having power involves taking it from someone else, and then using it to dominate and prevent others from gaining it. In politics, those who control resources and decision-making have power over those without. When people are denied access to important resources like land, health care, and jobs, power over perpetuates inequality, injustice, and poverty.

In the absence of alternative models and relationships, people repeat the power over pattern in their personal relationships, communities, and institutions. This is also true of people who come from a marginalized or powerless group. When they gain power in leadership positions, they sometimes imitate the oppressor. For this reason, advocates cannot expect that the experience of being excluded prepares people to become democratic leaders. New forms of leadership and decision-making must be explicitly defined, taught, and rewarded in order to promote more democratic forms of power. Practitioners and academics have searched for more collaborative ways of exercising and using power. Three alternatives—power with, power to, and power within—offer positive ways of expressing power that create the possibility of forming more equitable relationships. By affirming people's capacity to act creatively, they provide some basic principles for constructing empowering strategies.

Power With

Power with has to do with finding common ground among different interests and building collective strength. This is based on mutual support, solidarity and collaboration, power with multiple individual talents, and knowledge. Power with can help build bridges across different interests to transform or reduce social conflict and promote equitable relations. Advocacy groups seek allies and build coalitions drawing on the notion of power with.

Power To

Power to refers to the unique potential of every person to shape his or her life and world. When based on mutual support, it opens up the possibilities of joint action or power with. Citizen education and leadership development for advocacy are based on the belief that each individual has the power to make a difference.

Power Within

Power within has to do with a person's sense of self-worth and self-knowledge; it includes an ability to recognize individual differences while respecting others. Power within is the capacity to imagine and have hope; it affirms the common human search for dignity and fulfillment. Many grassroots efforts use individual storytelling and reflection to help people affirm personal worth and recognize their power to and power with. Both these forms of power are referred to as agency—the ability to act and change the world—by scholars writing about development and social change.

See also Jo Rowlands' book *Questioning Empowerment: Working with Women in Honduras* (1997, page 13) published by Oxfam which also covers these forms of **power.**

ASSIGNMENT

Outcomes: at the end of these sessions, participants should be able to write an essay of one or one and a half pages long.

Facilitated Activities:

- Describe their organization and the kind of work it does.
- Explain how this work enhances activism and what values are required to carry it out.
- Interview at least three leaders in their organizations, at least one must be a woman, and record their views on how they see the organization effecting change.

Reflections on the Module

This activism module laid the foundation for participants to embrace a new way of sharing, learning, and developing. It allowed them to engage in an education journey that was a shared experience rather than the individual one which is a common practice in the established education institutions. Drawing from their own experiences and using that as a starting point of engaging with theoretical and academic knowledge became the new challenge. This allowed them to understand their world better, to effect changes with ideas that came from them, and to embark on an activism that was value-based and principled. And it was the field work module, which they did simultaneously, that exposed participants to real challenges of people in vulnerable political and economic situations.

Reflections on the Work of the Workers' College: As an Organization for Social Change in a Society Trying to Renew Itself

Any organization claiming to fight for social change, should reflect that change or at least elements of the change sought in its own vision, governance structure, staff, ethos, and activities. Initially as a trade union education organization and then in 2000 including community organizations as part of its constituency, the college situated itself as an alternate education organization to that of the mainstream institutions. This immediately posed two major questions: who will fund the college, and will its education courses be recognized?

As the college was established in 1992/3, it was almost the dawn of a negotiated settlement between the apartheid state and the liberation movements. With the ushering of a democratic state, the opportunity arose to

MODULE II

hold the state responsible for developing the capacities of civil society organizations so that they could participate effectively as social partners in building the new society. And just as the state subsidized higher education for its citizens or at least those who could access it, similarly we held the state responsible for subsidizing the education of the working class.

But the greatest challenge for any organization or individual, for that matter, that sees itself bringing about radical change to a society, a world that is so fundamentally skewed, is to ensure that it does not get sucked into the very system it is fighting. Institutionalization is the process of co-opting organizations, and individuals into the status quo. Then you are made to believe that you are given the space and your democratic right to present a different opinion, a different world view, but all that happens is that it is accommodated within the dominant reality.

Participants who came onto the college's programs, came from organizations that purported to fight against injustices and advocated for radical change. These organizations included trade unions, community-based organizations, NGOs, and the like, who were steeped in fighting the cause, the struggle, on the front line, namely, where the injustices, exploitation, and oppressive realities were taking place. As a result, they were sucked into fighting these realities quite often in the same manner and with the same tools used by those who maintain the status quo. The college, like other education organizations, was removed from this front line. So it could afford to experiment with the way in which it structured itself, the kind of ethos and value system that it practised in doing its work and was able to continuously reflect on itself critically, its work, and its staff. As a result of this dynamic, there was always tension between the organizations in the front line and the college, even though representatives from these organizations sat on the governance structures of the college.

Finally, it must be said that students in higher education institutions in South Africa are questioning the continuation of what is viewed as a çolonized, education system that still advances a world view, a value system, a cultural and historical reality that does not represent the majority of the people in the country. In fact, such education is designed to perpetuate a denial of any other form of world view. Alternate education organizations that challenge the status quo, the dominant world view, are few and far between because to survive you must conform.

CHILE

Breaking Down Barriers and Strengthening Indigenous Culture and Language—The Role of PLAR

After seventeen years of bloody military dictatorship in which civil and human rights were restricted, a treaty was signed in 1989, signalling a return to democracy. The presidential candidate of the new democratic coalition signed an agreement with Indigenous peoples to design a new Indigenous law that would favour the individual and collective rights of the Indigenous population. The Indigenous associations and communities were organized under the legal wing of this new law, which also created the rural sectors of the Indigenous population.

This process was also carried out in urban centres, giving special legal status to Indigenous people residing in cities. In 1995 the Mapuche Indigenous Association **Taiñ Adkimn** was born, made up of young people, adults and children, all of Mapuche origin, who after four generations of forced migration settled in the metropolitan region, one of the largest cities in Chile where there are characteristics of stigmatization, discrimination, and uprooting of the Indigenous territories from the south of Chile.

Considering all this, **Taiñ Adkimn** has set its goals as follows:

Objective: To contribute to the improvement of living conditions and good living *(Kume Mogen)*, through the full exercise of the rights of Indigenous peoples, as well as the preservation, restoration, and increase in their economic, social, territorial, political, and cultural patrimony.

Vision: Recognizing that we live and dwell in a multicultural society, the Indigenous world must have the opportunity to recover and transmit the cultural knowledge bequeathed by generations, of which Indigenous peoples are the exclusive keepers/owners. This knowledge must be present in all activities of the Indigenous population and be recognized and respected by civil society in general.

Mission: To provide ancestral knowledge of Indigenous peoples in order to improve the quality of life, strengthening ancestral healing practices, revitalizing the cultural identity of Indigenous youth and adults, and establishing alliances with public and private organizations and institutions. Programs and other activities are designed with the purpose

MODULE II

of creating networks of support, with universities, Indigenous communities in the south of Chile, organizations, and associations in Santiago.

During the last decades, there have been a series of regulatory, legal, social, economic, and cultural changes that have ignored Indigenous peoples and their role as key players in the processes of change that affect our country in its development.

Despite these challenges, the most relevant milestone was the proclamation of the "Indigenous Law No. 19,253," in the year 1994, which recognizes the ethnicities of the country as well as the state's duty through its institutions to respect, protect, and promote the development of Indigenous peoples, their cultures, families, and communities, taking appropriate measures for such purposes and protecting the lands of Indigenous peoples to ensure their proper development, ecological balance, and promote their expansion.

In 2008 the ratification of Convention 169 also represents a substantive step forward in recognizing the status of people, noting further in Article 6 that in implementing the provisions of this Convention, governments shall:

1. Consult the concerned Indigenous peoples, through appropriate procedures and in particular through their representative institutions, whenever legislative or administrative measures are envisaged that may directly affect them.
2. Establish the means by which the peoples concerned may participate freely, at least to the same extent as other sectors of the population, and at all levels in decision-making in elected institutions and administrative and other bodies responsible for policies and programs that concern them.
3. To establish the means for the full development of the institutions and initiatives of those peoples and in appropriate cases provide the necessary resources for this purpose.

Finally, in May 2016, the "Indigenous Constituent Process" was initiated, which is carried out in a complementary way to the general constituent process in order to ensure a participatory process of their collective and individual rights. In order to follow up and support this process, a consultative and follow-up council was created, composed of representatives of international organizations, such as the United Nations

Development Programme (UNDP), ILO, UN, UNICEF, among others, in addition to two advisors from the National Indigenous Development Corporation (CONADI), and members of the inter-ministerial committee on Indigenous processes. However, different Indigenous organizations have criticized the process for failing to comply with the standards established in Article 6 of ILO Convention 169 on mechanisms for consultation and Indigenous representation.

All of the above becomes an important incentive for the Indigenous communities that inhabit this territory to commit ourselves to seek new mechanisms of recognition, visibility, and positioning of Indigenous peoples. In this sense, the Mapuche Indigenous community **Taiñ Adkimn** cannot be the exception. We have proposed to be an important agent of social change, "thus committing itself to fulfill its mission, in the promotion of the traditional values of pluralism, freedom of conscience, tolerance, and non-discrimination," from a democratic position and respectful of diversity, seeking mechanisms that promote true multiculturalism, contributing to the strengthening and development of ancestral knowledge and in the fields of education and health of cultures of Indigenous peoples, playing an essential role not only in the academic debate but also in the national debate. This implies an articulating role among the strategic actors of this process: Indigenous peoples, academics, and policy makers.

Taking into account the mission of our community, the alliance that was created with the Indigenous International RPL Collective has allowed us to achieve autonomy in our decisions, carrying out various activities in a collaborative and sustainable manner. The development of the **Taiñ Adkimn** community has enabled us through the numerous RPL symposiums, training of our leaders and members of the community, to be inserted in the programs of the University of Chile with courses designed and implemented by the **Taiñ Adkimn** members of the Collective.

Currently we are members of the Commission of Indigenous Peoples of the University of Chile, made up of representatives of the academic units that compose it, in order to contribute to the generation and strengthening of new initiatives related to positioning this issue in different formative expressions, research, and dissemination. We also aspire to have a voice in its statutory and normative provisions, where it is necessary to contribute in three dimensions: a) In the field of research and

MODULE II

development of new areas of knowledge, b) On the process of multicultural public policies, and c) The generation of models of intercultural management with interdisciplinary vision, among other objectives.

Taiñ Adkimn in recent years has been an active participant in the design of new Indigenous policies, where its members have participated actively in the different instances of dialogue, participation, and strengthening for a new Indigenous policy.

For our community to be part of the International Indigenous RPL Collective, it means a great support, strengthening, and development toward a new perspective on how to build a new Indigenous policy related to spiritual healing, to strengthening individual, collective, and institutional capacities.

The International Indigenous RPL Collective has collaborated and been an active entity in the design of a new methodology with Indigenous relevance in the daily work of **Taiñ Adkimn**. Its leaders have been strengthened by this alliance, which has allowed us to have a new perspective on the development of these new government policies. This strengthening has been carried out through exchanges of experiences between both institutions of leaders and young people of this Mapuche community which has substantially improved **Taiñ Adkimn**'s management in recent years.

This joint work venture between **Taiñ Adkimn** and the International Indigenous RPL Collective for more than twelve years has been recognized by the Canadian Embassy in Chile which has become a collaborator and facilitator in this relationship between both organizations, a fact manifested in the recognition given to the Lonko (leaders) of the community by Mr. David Johnston, Governor General of Canada.

Today we can affirm that the **Taiñ Adkimn** Indigenous Association has become a reference for the work of the multiple Indigenous activities/affairs that exist between Chile and Canada.

Our experience with PLAR began in 2003 when **Taiñ Adkimn** partnered with FNTI on the Tyendinaga Mohawk Territory in Canada on a project funded by the Indigenous Peoples Partnership Program of the Canadian Government. We began to implement portfolio development with our community members. In phase I we were introduced to the basic principles of the portfolio development process within an Indigenous framework and eighteen members of our community took part in the training. Phase II was based on advanced applications of PLAR and portfolio development as a tool for healing and unburdening. The culturally relevant portfolio process was very helpful because it demonstrated respect for the individual and his or her community. It also helped identify the strengths and gifts of Indigenous people who have been suppressed and repressed for generations. The portfolio helped to break down barriers and to build self-esteem, self-confidence, and reduce the negative impact of discrimination and colonization.

Taiñ Adkimn also introduced the portfolio development process to Indigenous people in rural communities in the south of Chile, in and around Temuco. In 2008 meetings were held with Indigenous leaders, political bodies, and community members. The meetings involved describing the culturally based portfolio process, its uses, and benefits in helping community members reach their education, training, employment, personal, and cultural goals. We visited three communities with a total of approximately 250 people participating in the sessions. There was a great deal of interest expressed by the people in the portfolio process. One of the major challenges was the lack of funding to implement portfolio development workshops for those people.

Taiñ Adkimn continues to be an active partner in the Collective and seeks to expand the practice of culturally respectful PLAR and portfolio development to our compañeros in other Indigenous Nations in Chile and throughout South America.

MODULE II

Mapuche Cosmovision and Circle of Life
Cosmovision Y Ciclo De La Vida Mapuche—Inglés

EL, he who establishes

ULCHA, Young woman

WIZUFE,
He who gives shape.

**KUME MONGE
WELL BEING**

AZ MONGEN,
Gives order to life

FUCHA, Elderly Woman

WECHE, Young man

GUNE
He who guides; gives guidance.

KUCHE, Elderly Man.

MODULE III

Training International Indigenous RPL Practitioners

Introduction

This module identifies the key functions of international Indigenous RPL practitioners in relation to the roles and responsibilities of advisor and assessor. It integrates principles and processes drawn from mainstream RPL practice with competencies, attitudes, beliefs, and values of Indigenous RPL practitioners. It does so in part by drawing on culturally based examples arising from three models of Indigenous RPL practice using portfolio development in their communities—the Coast Salish, Haudenosaunee, and Inuit which can be found in module IV.

Module Outcomes

Upon successful completion of this module, participants should be able to:

- Discuss the importance of creating RPL and portfolio development processes that are respectful of their Indigenous heritage and the needs of their community.
- Outline at least six principles of Indigenous RPL practice.
- Assemble a personal portfolio which reflects their own unique gifts, skills, and experiences as an Indigenous person.

Key Competencies of the Indigenous RPL Practitioner

CREATING A PORTFOLIO PROCESS TO COMPLEMENT INDIGENOUS TEACHINGS: BASIC PRINCIPLES

The Indigenous portfolio process is grounded in the belief, expression, understanding, and application of the relationship with one's self, one's family and community, and with the land, language, and culture. Key factors to consider include:

- Create a portfolio development process in respectful consultation with local Indigenous communities
- Display evidence of direct and indirect experiential methods that reinforce Indigenous ways of knowing and being
- Demonstrate local Indigenous participation in portfolio course development, by engaging with fluent speakers, community resource persons, and culturally relevant teachings
- Provide examples of strategies for integrating Indigenous ways of knowing (storytelling)
- Having elders and/or traditional knowledge keepers teach
- Participation in community and cultural activities
- Preparing and sharing traditional food (feasting)
- Participating in learning circles
- Promote traditional land-based learning
- Learning and practising cultural protocols (e.g. acknowledgement of traditional territory)

The next section of the manual contains an evidence-based portfolio development process enabling Indigenous practitioners to compare their skills and knowledge to those of the Indigenous RPL practitioner.

This self-assessment has been designed to help you determine your level of competence in relation to four of the key functions of international Indigenous RPL practice.

The scale contains critical components drawn from mainstream RPL practice which have been integrated with attitudes, beliefs, and values of Indigenous RPL practitioners.

MODULE III

The assessment process enables you to take an active role in assessing, documenting, and monitoring your ongoing development as an Indigenous RPL advisor.

The self-assessment should:

- Encourage and support you in taking responsibility for assessing your own learning
- Assist you in assessing your level of competence as an advisor and helping you identify gaps in your skills and knowledge
- Assist you in focusing on the Indigenous RPL advisor competencies and deciding which of them to pursue by providing evidence of your competence in those areas and building your own portfolio
- Create the design of an individualized learning plan based on your previous experiences and learning related to the competencies enabling you to strengthen existing skills and knowledge and to fill any gaps in your approach

The starting point is a thoughtful, honest self-assessment of your level of competence in relation to the advisor competencies. The checklist has been designed to help you compare your skills and knowledge to the advisor competencies and their performance indicators. Please check the level of performance which you believe best describes your competence in each of the areas.

Scale

| 0 | 1 | 2 | 3 | 4 | 5 |

RATING

    0 — Have no experience with this
    1 — Have observed this or been oriented to this
    2 — Can participate in and assist with this
    3 — Can do this with minimum assistance
    4 — Can successfully do this without assistance
    5 — Can successfully do this without assistance and lead others in doing it.

Carefully review each of the four Indigenous advisor competencies and their performance indicators. Using the self-assessment scale, record what you think is your present level of competence. Make notes of possible sources of evidence in the right-hand column of any particular tasks, projects, responsibilities, courses, training programs, self-directed study in which you have participated that may help you to demonstrate competence. You may find that one piece of evidence is strong enough to demonstrate competence in more than one function. However, you will probably need more than one piece of evidence to demonstrate competence in any one competency area. Providing diverse sources of evidence to demonstrate your competence is a critical element of the RPL process.

After completing the self-assessment activity, it may be a good idea to take some time to review the entire advisor's manual. Pay particular attention to those benchmarks for which you consistently rated yourself as being able to perform the competency with minimum assistance and/or without assistance. Such ratings indicate that these are the areas on which to focus in generating various forms of evidence to support your claim that you possess the required advisor skills and knowledge.

Collecting Evidence to Support Competence

Providing appropriate sources and types of documentation (evidence) to support one's claim of competence is a key component of RPL. Evidence generally falls into two categories: direct and indirect.

Direct evidence refers to products, reports, plans, and performances that you have created and produced. In most cases direct evidence is the

MODULE III

strongest evidence to support your claim that you really do have the skills and knowledge that you say you have in relation to the Indigenous advisor competencies. Try to collect as much direct evidence related to the competencies as possible in support of your claim of competence.

Indirect evidence generally refers to information about you and your achievements/competencies. Examples of indirect evidence include letters of validation written on your behalf by employers, supervisors, co-workers, members of professional associations, formal job evaluations, awards, commendations.

In many cases, direct evidence or observation of one's skills and knowledge may not be possible due to cost, confidentiality, lack of time, etc. When it is not possible or realistic to provide direct evidence to support one's claim of competence indirect sources of evidence may be used. A flexible combination of direct and indirect evidence is highly desirable and commonly used as an integral part of the RPL assessment process.

Remember that throughout the assessment process emphasis should be placed on ensuring that diverse sources of evidence are used, that is, **at least three sources for each of the major functions and activities and their accompanying performance indicators.** The example which follows demonstrates the principle of triangulation of evidence related to Function #1—Indigenous Leadership and Facilitation.

EVIDENCE → Letter of Validation from Chief and Council commending you on your workshop and dedication to cultural teachings

FUNCTION 1
Indigenous Leadership and Facilitation

EVIDENCE → Agenda from community workshop on Indigenous ceremonies and healing practices you delivered

Summary of feedback from participants in community workshop on Indigenous ceremonies and healing practices ← EVIDENCE

Self-Assessment Scale

INDIGENOUS RPL PRACTITIONER
ADVISORS OF RPL CANDIDATES
ESSENTIAL SKILLS AND KNOWLEDGE OF RPL ADVISOR

The Indigenous RPL practitioner must have strong relationship building skills which include respect, reciprocity, creativity, collaboration, innovation, and demonstrated ability to engage with others by building a climate of mutual trust and authenticity. The Indigenous RPL practitioner must strive to model a constant state of reflection and self-awareness that leads to deeper learning. The Indigenous RPL practitioner must also develop a personal portfolio using the following questions as guidelines:

1. Who are you? What experiences have you had in your life that have shaped you? What have you learned in your life that might not show up in your resume? What are your values and strengths?

2. Where do you come from? Who are your role models? What have you learned from them? What traditional knowledge do you hold? What is your relationship with your culture? What is your sacred connection to the land?

3. Where are you going? What is the dream that is calling you? How do you want to give back?

MODULE III

RPL ADVISOR COMPETENCES AND PERFORMANCE INDICATORS

ROLES AND RESPONSIBILITIES

1. Indigenous leadership and facilitation
2. Informing and selecting RPL candidates
3. Assisting candidates to gain access to education and training programs and employment
4. Supporting candidates to complete education and training programs and occupations and helping them identify next steps in learning plans.

SCALE	0	1	2	3	4	5

0 Have no experience with this
1 Have observed this or been oriented to this
2 Can participate in and assist with this
3 Can do this with minimum assistance
4 Can successfully do this without assistance
5 Can successfully do this without assistance and lead others in doing it

ROLES AND RESPONSIBILITIES – INDIGENOUS RPL ADVISOR

FUNCTION I: Indigenous Leadership and Facilitation

ACTIVITY	PERFORMANCE INDICATORS	0	1	2	3	4	5	POSSIBLE EVIDENCE
1. The relationship between the RPL practitioner and the candidate is critical in developing an effective and wholistic portfolio process within a cultural context. The Indigenous RPL Practitioner must be capable of establishing a positive relationship based on respect and unconditional acceptance of the culture, life circumstances and language of the candidate	- explain key issues, milestones of Indigenous history and discuss contemporary issues - demonstrate knowledge and experience working with Indigenous communities - recognize and value diversity - identify distinct Indigenous healing practices, ceremonies, values, beliefs - demonstrate respect for Indigenous ways of knowing and being and cultural sensitivity - implement and support Indigenous teachings e.g. land based learning - demonstrate ability to hold space with sensitivity when working with complex issues - demonstrate intuition, flexibility, collaboration, tolerance with others							

The International Indigenous RPL Practitioner Manual

SCALE	
0	Have no experience with this
1	Have observed this or been oriented to this
2	Can participate in and assist with this
3	Can do this with minimum assistance
4	Can successfully do this without assistance
5	Can successfully do this without assistance and lead others in doing it

FUNCTION II: Informing and Selecting RPL Candidates

ACTIVITY	PERFORMANCE INDICATORS	0	1	2	3	4	5	POSSIBLE EVIDENCE
1. Help candidates make informed decisions about education and employment opportunities based on their life and employment goals.	- demonstrate basic interviewing skills - apply group facilitation skills within a cultural context e.g. learning circles, story telling - describe personal theory of working with others as a helper - list attitudes needed for effective advising							
2. Work collaboratively with candidates to help them overcome barriers of time and place using Indigenous teachings and ceremonies enabling them to pursue learning goals.	- outline ways in which language and cultural teachings may be used to assist candidates - develop mutually respectful relationships with candidates e.g. acceptance, empathy, tolerance, non-judgmental - communicate with candidates using Indigenous teachings, values, ceremonies to help them develop confidence and the strength to pursue demands of education/training programs, occupational requirements - recognize feelings of uncertainty and anxiety by responding sensitively to concerns related to returning to formal study or work.							

MODULE III

SCALE	0	1	2	3	4	5
0	Have no experience with this
1	Have observed this or been oriented to this
2	Can participate in and assist with this
3	Can do this with minimum assistance
4	Can successfully do this without assistance
5	Can successfully do this without assistance and lead others in doing it

ACTIVITY	PERFORMANCE INDICATORS	0	1	2	3	4	5	POSSIBLE EVIDENCE
	- demonstrate support, encouragement by responding promptly to requests for information about education, training and occupational requirements							
	- schedule information sessions at times and locations convenient for candidates							
	- explore with candidates individually and in small groups personal, cultural, education and training goals and needs							
	- assist candidates to assume as much responsibility as possible for making decisions about whether to pursue specific cultural, education, training and employment goals or to explore other options							
	- assist candidates to formally register for specific education, training and employment programs by helping them obtain the necessary materials and resources							

The International Indigenous RPL Practitioner Manual

SCALE	0	1	2	3	4	5
0	Have no experience with this
1	Have observed this or been oriented to this
2	Can participate in and assist with this
3	Can do this with minimum assistance
4	Can successfully do this without assistance
5	Can successfully do this without assistance and lead others in doing it

FUNCTION III: Assisting Candidates To Gain Access To Education and Training Programs and Employment

ACTIVITY	PERFORMANCE INDICATORS	0	1	2	3	4	5	POSSIBLE EVIDENCE
1. RPL practitioners help candidates to gain access to education and training programs and employment opportunities by developing portfolios which are based on their cultural teachings and community needs and circumstances	- describe the Indigenous, portfolio-assisted RPL process - implement portfolio development steps in collaboration with RPL candidates - explore with RPL candidates their personal, cultural and work related learning related to candidate goals - facilitate individual and small group portfolio development classes, seminars, workshops based on Indigenous teachings - assist candidates to identify and document skills, knowledge and attitudes related to education, training and occupational requirements - assist candidates to prepare and submit portfolios for assessment							

MODULE III

SCALE	0	1	2	3	4	5
0	Have no experience with this
1	Have observed this or been oriented to this
2	Can participate in and assist with this
3	Can do this with minimum assistance
4	Can successfully do this without assistance
5	Can successfully do this without assistance and lead others in doing it

FUNCTION IV: Supporting Candidates To Complete Education And Training Programs And Occupations And Helping Them Identify Next Steps In Learning Plans.

ACTIVITY	PERFORMANCE INDICATORS	0	1	2	3	4	5	POSSIBLE EVIDENCE
1. Review learning plans with candidates to determine future goals, strategies and resources	- review education, training and employment experience with candidates - collaborate with candidates to create strategic plans for ongoing learning activities							
2. Collaborate with candidates to gain credit and recognition from a variety of sources enabling them to receive academic credentials or recognition for occupational skills and knowledge and cultural teachings	- develop strategies to maintain regular contact with candidates - provide ongoing support reaching out, if necessary to candidates							

The International Indigenous RPL Practitioner Manual

Sample of a Possible Portfolio Framework

Page 1   Title Page

Portfolio of Prior Learning Related to International Indigenous RPL Advisor Competencies

Presented by:

Submitted to:

Modules for which RPL Credits are Requested:
- A. Function I-Indigenous Leadership and Facilitation
- B. Function II-(title)
- C. Function III-(title)
- D. Function IV-(title)

Date:

Page 2   Table of Contents

TABLE OF CONTENTS

1. Narrative Related to Indigenous RPL Advisor Competencies

2. Resume

3. Competency Areas for which PLAR Credits are Requested

   ➢ Title of Function e.g. Function #1 – Informing and Selecting Candidates
   Evidence to Demonstrate Competence

   ➢ Title of Function – e.g. Function #2 – Assisting Candidates to Gain Access to Learning/Occupational Program
   Evidence to Demonstrate Competence

   ➢ Title of Function e.g. Function #3, etc.
   Evidence to Demonstrate Competence

Page 3   Narrative on Involvement in Adult Learning Activities Related to Indigenous RPL Advisor Competencies

The narrative should provide the context for your request for RPL credits. Use the following questions as a guide. Who are you? What life experiences have helped shape you? What have you learned in your life that might not show up on your resume? What are your values and strengths?

Where do you come from? Who are your role models? What have you learned from them? What Traditional Knowledge do you hold? What is your relationship with your culture? What is your sacred connection to the land? Where are you going? What is the dream that is calling you? How do you want to give back?

Page 4   Resume

Page 5   Competency Areas for which RPL Credits are Requested

Title of Function e.g. Function #1 – Indigenous Leadership and Facilitation

Evidence to Demonstrate Competence

Page 6   Competency Areas for which RPL Credits are Requested

Title of Function – e.g. Function #2 – Informing and Selecting RPL Candidates

Evidence to Demonstrate Competence

Page 7   Competency Areas for which RPL Credits are Requested
Title of Function etc.

Title of Function e.g. Function #3
Assisting Candidates to Gain Access to, etc.

Evidence to Demonstrate Competence

MODULE IV

Examples of Diverse Indigenous Applications of RPL and Portfolio Development

Introduction

This module examines examples of the application of the portfolio development process from three Indigenous cultures: the Coast Salish, the Haudenosaunee, and the Inuit.

The three portfolio processes are rooted in cultural teachings and symbols: The Canoe of Life (Coast Salish), The Longhouse (Haudenosaunee), and the Igloo of Life (Inuit).

The module also outlines a set of generic guidelines and principles intended to be used as a framework to help Indigenous cultures to create portfolio processes which are respectful of their culture, teachings, language, and community needs.

Module Outcomes

Upon successful completion of this module, participants should be able to:

- Recognize the importance of creating a portfolio process that reflects their unique cultural teachings which supports the needs of their community.
- List the basic principles and processes which constitute a culturally respectful portfolio development process and framework.
- Create, with support, a basic outline of key components of a portfolio process reflective of the teachings and world view of their culture.

Creating a Portfolio Process to Complement Indigenous Teachings—Principles and Processes

THE CANOE OF LIFE

Many thanks to the Elders in Residence at VIU, who provide ongoing guidance for this model and in sharing the teachings and wisdom from traditional Coast Salish Nations. Indigenous portfolio development courses must be collaboratively developed with local Indigenous communities in order to hold to the traditional teachings of the land and language on which the course is to be taught.

We especially would like to acknowledge and thank Elders Xulsimalt Gary Manson and Ctasia Geraldine Manson from Snuneymuxw First Nation who co-taught the courses and who guided Janet Sinclair and Brian Walker in developing the Canoe of Life model.

Ideally, elders or traditional knowledge keepers would co-teach the portfolio development course in order to address the issues of the four Rs*—respect, relevance, reciprocity, and responsibility. *(Kirkness and Barnhardt, 1991) First Nations and Higher Education: The four Rs—**respect, relevance, reciprocity, and responsibility.**

In developing a framework for a portfolio development process which respects one's culture and traditions as an Indigenous person, it is important to recognize that you will need to guide learners through a process of identity and cultural awareness that begins with connecting to the land.

Important factors to consider in this consultation process include land and language, who am I, where I come from, where am I going, and giving back.

Land and Language—helping students to connect to the land and identifying the importance of the relationship between the land and language. Students may be asked to spend time alone on the land and then to write a story on their relationship with the land as an Indigenous person. Often in this process students will connect more directly with their inner selves and the land they come from. Elders stress the importance of realizing that this is an important first step for students.

Who I Am—Standing in my strength, students begin to more clearly identify and articulate values they possess, their strengths, interests, and gifts.

MODULE IV

Where I Come From—Students begin to identify their origins more clearly in terms of land, language, culture, community, elders, family, role models and traditional knowledge based on their life experiences. Processes and activities that help students address these issues include looking at their family tree, community, role models and traditional teachings. You may organize trips to sacred sites and visit other places in their community that can help them learn the history and struggles of their people. To assist them in answering these questions, you can suggest they meet with an elder to discuss their history and traditions and then to write a reflection paper on their learning that took place. This can be a powerful experience for many learners.

Where I Am Going—Walking in my strength. Students begin to explore options and choices based on their talents and gifts, planning in the present, and setting goals for their future. They create education and career plans that can help them connect to employment possibilities by taking stock of themselves and their hopes and dreams for the future. As part of this process they may also interview other students and employers, and they may sit in on classes to get a realistic sense of the choices they are making.

Giving Back—Sharing who I am and identifying ways in which my strengths, talents, and gifts may contribute to the growth and development of others. The guiding principles in this process include respect, gratitude, kindness, reciprocity, and giving.

In the first meeting with students, there are some basic questions that may be asked including the following:

- 1st Activity: Who are you? – Students are asked to answer this question on their own and then share it with another person. What have you learned in your life that didn't show up on you resume?

- 2nd Activity: Where do you come from? – In pairs, then in groups of four, then groups of eight, and then with the entire group, students share their responses to this question.

- 3rd Activity: Where are you going? – Individually think about this question and then find a partner and share your responses to the question. Where do you see yourself in five years? Discuss ways in which you can give back.

The International Indigenous RPL Practitioner Manual

The Indigenous portfolio process is grounded in the belief, expression, understanding, and application of the relationship with one's self, one's family and community, and with the land. Throughout the Indigenous learning recognition portfolio course, students discover who they are, where they come from, and where they are going; they develop a way to tell their own story. This course facilitates change, invited growth, and reframes challenges from the past, always looking for strengths, knowledge, and lived experience which can transfer to new learning situations. Portfolio development can be adapted to a variety of contexts, recognizing that adults already have knowledge, skills, attitudes, and abilities, and can result in establishing or confirming goals and creating learning plans that lead to success in their educational journey. The Canoe of Life model, developed in collaboration with Coast Salish elders, is a process of personal reflection and assessment of prior learning that leads to the development of a portfolio. Simply, the Canoe of Life model is based upon the process of understanding who I am (Canoe), where I come from (Cedar Tree), and where I am going (Eagle).

OVERVIEW

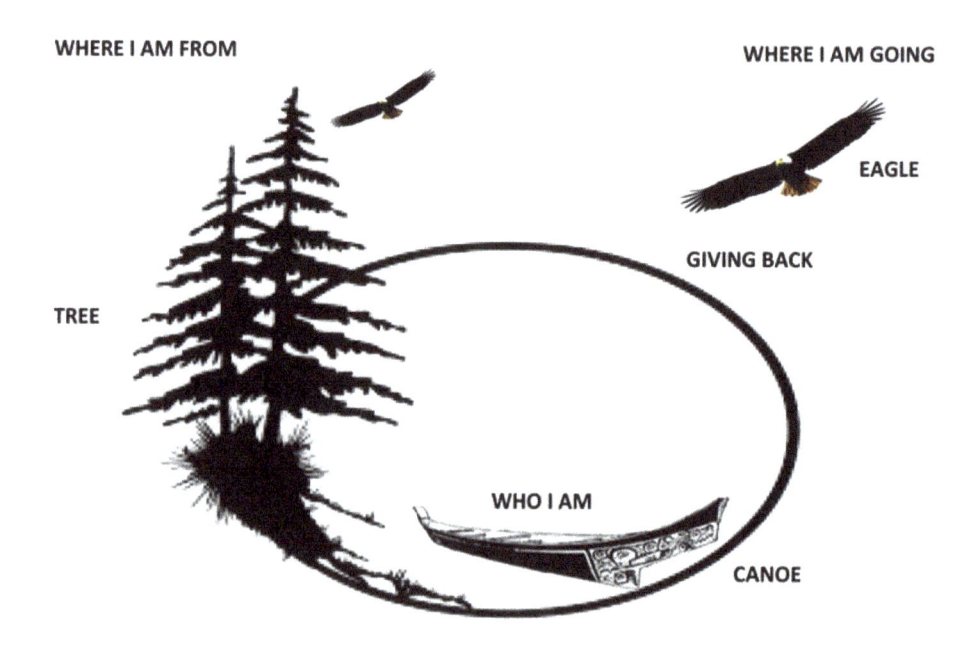

MODULE IV

WHO I AM

The traditional canoe is built from material specially selected for strength, flexibility, and beauty. The precision of the craftsman/carver forms the canoe into shape. Traditional medicine (such as cedar) keeps the canoe healthy, and the integrity of the canoe remains intact. The canoe building process starts with the search of the right tree in the forest and involves giving thanks to the tree. The metaphor of the canoe teaches us about knowing ourselves and maintaining balance: values, strengths, skills, attitudes, and our purpose.

Knowing yourself and your purpose: An important first step in personal growth comes through an exploration of the self to determine who you are and where you came from. What are your personal values? We reflect upon these things, looking for our strengths and skills, remembering our values, and honouring our attitudes. Knowing ourselves and our purpose means to explore the experiences we have lived thus far to locate what we know and what we can do. Reframing the past in personal ways allows for new awareness and growth. We get in touch with our personal qualities and values. From this exploration we can begin to recognize our purpose in living: what is it we want to do with our lives in relation to the world in which we live?

Knowing your strengths: Strength comes from many things—physical abilities included. Strength can be a learned skill that help us perform well in our lives. Strength can be ways of being, often originating out of our core values. For example, patience is often a great strength when used appropriately. Strength may arise out of past challenges or personal defeat. Often, we do not know our strengths. They remain buried beneath a pile of past unresolved experience. What did you gain from that tough experience? An honest examination of our strengths puts us in touch with our abilities and wisdom.

Self-discipline: There is an old saying: "It is not so much what happens to us that determines who we become; it is how we deal with what happens to us." This is true measure of who we become. Without self-discipline we are powerless in the face of our emotions and our thoughts. Rather than keeping us in control and thinking clearly, we react instantly without the ability to stop ourselves. We make messes and repeat past mistakes rather than side-stepping challenges with tact, wit, and grace. Self-discipline allows us to consider our intentions, manage our emotions, find alternative solutions, and remain healthy and in control of our lives. How disciplined are you? What keeps you from being more disciplined?

Maintaining balance: There are many pulls and pushes in our lives. We are called upon to respond and react to an ever-growing list of demands, stimuli, and challenges that distract and overwhelm the senses. The Wellness Wheel helps us to, at least, know the components of a holistic life, but living a well-balanced life takes commitment, discipline, and self-awareness. Maintaining balance becomes empowerment through the experience of living through the challenges and succeeding—each step forward builds confidence and resilience.

WHERE I COME FROM

Family: Our grandparents and our parents (and their brothers and sisters, uncles and aunts, grandparents, and cousins galore), this is our family. The who of our family, as it relates to biology and heritage, is often unexplored (even unknown). What we were given from our families is also often unexplored. Families can take many shapes and forms. "Who raised us?" is often a question that brings many replies. Who are our role models? Therefore, families are more than shared genetics and the names that they are called. They are a collective, sometimes a collective of strangers. And as kin, they are connected by attitudes and values and shared experiences—sometimes in opposition, sometimes in harmony. What is your heritage? Who are your kin? What did they teach you? How do you feel about that? These are the questions which begin our exploration.

Community Support: The notion of community has evolved past the point of person, place, or thing. Communities exist for many reasons, including location, affiliation, purpose, blood relation and culture, shared values, history, characteristics, interests, or even emotional connection. Some require special membership. Others are formed simply out of the need to share ideas, information, and resources. Virtual communities are the wave of the present. What communities have you been a part of (and are now a part of)? What learning came from that participation? What do you offer to your communities? What support do you receive? These are the questions that begin an exploration of community influence and support.

MODULE IV

Culture and Language: Where do I come from? What mix of race fills my lineage? What was the influence of my traditional culture, and how was it expressed and lived? What other cultures influence my life? How has the virtual world of technology influenced my cultural identity? These are the questions that help us understand the cultural influences that shape our existence and our past. How have all my cultural experiences been operationalized (lived) this far in my life? An honest and open look at how we feel and think (and act) in relation to our cultural identification helps us to identify skills, knowledge, and attitudes that may form the foundation for lifelong learning.

Land: What is my connection to the land? What are my traditional teachings? What is my relationship with all living things?

Integrity: What you do when no one is watching makes up your ethics—your code of living. How truthful are you with yourself and with others? To have integrity is to live in harmony with one's self, balanced in a truthful understanding and a personal accountability of our physical, emotional, spiritual, and intellectual worlds. When we demonstrate integrity in all that we do, we can count on ourselves, and others can count on us.

Gratitude: Living a life of appreciative gratitude is to value and respect who we are and what we do in our lives. It is often harder than it sounds and often easier to do with others. To show self-gratitude is to acknowledge our good traits and to celebrate ourselves with kindness and appreciation, patting ourselves on the back rather than kicking our own butt. What do you appreciate about your life? What traits bring you the most self-satisfaction? Such gratitude for self allows us to face challenges with unyielding faith in what we can do.

WHERE AM I GOING?

Direction/Goals: Where do you want to go in life? What do want to do? Our direction comes from the goals we set, which help set our future. When our direction/goals are tied to our heart's desire, more passion and faith are generated and our chances for success are increased. To not believe in yourself is to remain empty of confidence and ripe for self-contempt and failure. To trust and believe in yourself allows for faith in your abilities and purpose and in who you are in this world. This allows others to see you as you see yourself and is a key component in personal development. What are your abilities? What is the dream that is calling you?

Finding Your Voice: This is not simply telling your story. Finding your voice allows you to answer questions and give opinions with confidence to interact with faith in your contribution, to reveal your mind and heart with passion, and integrity and to respond to the moment without doubt or fear. Finding your voice allows you to express your truth as it evolves before you. Finding your voice allows you to connect with others and to your reason for being. It is a voice of confidence and self-esteem that arises out of pride and love for self, knowing that you have something of value to offer. What keeps your voice quiet? Where does your voice come from?

Telling Your Story: Each story is unique. Telling it properly depends upon how well one understands the truth about life. Who are you? Where are you from? What do you believe? When done with clarity, telling your story helps identify talents, skills, values, interests, as well as to name limitations and fears. Each person sees the world through their own eyes, but to tell your story properly depends upon how open and honest one has been examining (writing) their script.

Giving Back: Reciprocity is an important part of living a balanced life in relationship with others and is one of the four Rs from the traditional way of being. Giving back to your family, community, and to the world for what it has given you, provides for the expression of your gratitude, appreciation, care, and connection. It fulfills an opportunity to live a life in balance with needs and the care of something beyond the self. Giving back brings satisfaction and depth of feeling and allows one's self to feel both valued and worthwhile. It enhances the self through the lived experience of reciprocity. Who gave to you? How will you give back or give forward?

MODULE IV

Coast Salish Canoe of Life Model of Portfolio Process

```
                    GIVING BACK
                   Sharing who I am
        HELPING                    SHARING

WHERE I AM GOING    LAND & LANGUAGE        WHO I AM
  Walking in my       this place          Standing in my
    strength         and people  RESPECT    strength

                                        THANKING
        KINDNESS
                    WHERE I COME
                       FROM
                    Land and Ancestry
```

To see self as a canoe allows for a meaningful examination of fit and purpose. It takes many things to make a canoe go, just as it takes many things to make a person successful in life:

- Many spirits shape, guide, and propel the canoe, just as there are many aspects to the self.
- We can be balanced, healthy and true like a canoe, when we make choices to learn and grow/change.
- We strengthen our personal foundation by learning about ourselves and our past and then by loving ourselves fully.
- The materials which make a canoe must have strength, integrity, and resiliency. Each living thing that becomes this sacred vessel gives itself for the good of the whole. The self can be constructed in such a way.
- It is through the craftsmanship of the carver that depth, texture, unity, and artistic expression (voice) emerge; each canoe is a living, breathing, sacred vessel of movement and precision. We can shape our personal development through the rafting of our choices, goals, and learned experiences.

- The canoe remains healthy and strong with careful attention to maintenance and care. The steering remains true when one has faith in their process and direction, paying careful attention to what is needed in the moment. The paddles remain in sync when there is successful coordination of a unified purpose. We keep the self in sync by committing to a healthy life of learning. The call remains true with careful attention to the moment. We make the right call in our personal development when our awareness and honest reflection supports the appropriate voice needed in the moment.

FEEDBACK FROM THE LEARNERS

"I really enjoyed the portfolio assignment. I discovered a lot about myself, and I still have more to discover and share. It was very therapeutic, and I suggest it to anyone who is struggling with making decisions or changes in their life. I found it helped me to determine what direction I will take in education."

"I loved the experience that I gained from writing my portfolio, and in retrospect I really appreciate the emotional feedback that I not only gained internally but also the changes that I have made within my own life. In particular, the one reference of the Canoe of Life I really feel that writing the portfolio has not only made myself take a lot of added baggage off my shoulders but also made me really look deeply into what is important. The Indigenous portfolio not only has made us look into our lives and look at what we can do to make changes but also has helped better us to specifically work with Indigenous people."

"I found the portfolio experience to be interesting and enlightening. It was emotional in a good way. It allowed me to highlight the life of my dear sister who passed away in April 2015. It was simple and not easy to do, and the results were wonderful once it was put together. Thank you for allowing me to be part of this healing process. Thank you for planting the seed of the Indigenous portfolio. I have now begun to dig and recover my own history and that of my ancestors. I am really excited about this process."

"I can't believe I learned about my own culture at university."

MODULE IV

The RPL practitioner reported, "I have seen transformational learning take place with the students doing the Indigenous portfolio work. I know this process has helped students get clearer on goals for their future, feel more self-confident, and gain a sense of cultural pride. For some students, this work is a reaffirmation of the cultural knowledge they have been taught, and for others this is a beginning point in their path of learning more about their culture. When the students are willing to put in the work, building an Indigenous portfolio can be a profound learning experience."

Long House

Janice Brant, a Mohawk scholar and educator, in her manual, "Utilizing Portfolio Development in Adult Basic Education" writes, "The role of the facilitator throughout the RPL process is to transfer responsibility to the group, creating learner empowerment. Learners must recognize that they are responsible for their own learning and begin to take ownership and control."

Janice created a portfolio process for Haudenosaunee adult learners on the Tyendinaga Mohawk Territory in Ontario, Canada. It was then offered at NokeeKwe Aboriginal Learning Centre in London, Ontario as a pilot project to test the manual. The facilitator was Bernice Ireland of the Oneida Nation. The learners were from many nations and both urban and rural communities. The process was intended to provide adults with the opportunity to explore and document their life experience and to recognize and value their accumulated skills and knowledge. This process was also aimed at empowering them by improving their self-image and self-confidence. Many of the learners needed assistance with basic literacy and numeracy skills which became the building blocks that would eventually help them pursue higher education and employment goals.

The use of the portfolio process with Haudenosaunee adult learners was designed to recognize their diverse life experiences by identifying and documenting the informal learning that arose from their relationship to self, family, clan, community, nation, confederacy, Creation, and universe. The portfolio process also provided a safe place in which cultural knowledge and practices could be shared and valued, often for the first time.

The portfolio process creates an environment in which multiple barriers to learning can be identified and addressed. It is also intended to stimulate reflective thinking and self-assessment, creating a climate in which adult learners are given the support and encouragement necessary for them to assume ownership and control over their own learning.

A HAUDENOSAUNEE ADULT LEARNER

In order to make PLA portfolio development models applicable in Haudenosaunee communities, it was first necessary to look at the Haudenosaunee adult learner, their culture, and world view.

Haudenosaunee is a name that people of the six Iroquois Nations used to refer to themselves. The six Iroquois or Haudenosaunee Nations are the Mohawk, Seneca, Onondoga, Oneida, Cayuga, and Tuscarora. The term Haudenosaunee comes from the Onondaga language. In the Mohawk language, Rotinonshon:ni is the term used.

The term Haudenosaunee has been most commonly understood to simply mean *the people of the longhouse.* In the broader meaning it describes *building an extended house or adding and extending the rafters of the longhouse.* The longhouse is the type of traditional dwelling of the Haudenosaunee people. They built and lived in these long structures that housed an extended family. The relationship of families in a longhouse began with a matriarch or clan mother, her daughters and their husbands, and her unmarried sons. They would all be of the same clan with the exception of the husbands. These houses could be extended to accommodate the additional members of the growing family.

In thinking about the meaning of the longhouse in Haudenosaunee culture in its broadest interpretation, Janice envisioned the longhouse or the extended house as a learner. More specifically, a person or human being with body, heart, mind, and spirit. These are the four aspects of the human being: physical, mental, emotional, and spiritual. The longhouse, like the human being is a house where our memories, feelings, life experiences, and all learning is processed and stored.

What is unique in this perspective is that as we move through the life cycle, we grow and change, continually building and extending the rafters of our house, metaphorically speaking. This growth that occurs begins and stems from our relationships to all things, beginning with self, family

MODULE IV

(fireside family), clan (extended family), community, nation, confederacy, Creation, and universe. These are the eight essential rafters, which represent our significant relationships within each life stage and the experience and learning that we gain through these relationships.

In making the PLA portfolio process relevant to Haudenosaunee adult learners, it was important to explore these eight segments or rafters in order to begin to document their accumulated learning, skills, and knowledge.

We included the teachings of the eight life stages: infant, toddler, child, youth or adolescent, adult, parent, grandparent and elder, by Silvia Maracle of Tyendinaga. Together with the eight rafters, what we saw is that regardless of where we are in the human life cycle, we can explore our individual learning through the experience of our relationships to self, family, clan, community, nation, confederacy, Creation and universe.

Equally important is the recognition and inclusion of the four aspects of the human being: physical, mental, emotional, and spiritual. It promotes awareness of self as a whole being. There is a well-defined recognition within Haudenosaunee philosophy that our basic human needs be fulfilled in all aspects of our being and that they are integral to our individual identity. The PLA portfolio process operates to include "our need to be seen, to be heard, to feel safe (to know others have faith and trust in us), to feel secure about and at peace with one's self, to belong and be allowed to take our place in the world, to be accepted for who we are, and to feel a sense of purpose and that our individual existence is beneficial" (*The Power Within People*, 1986: Antone, Miller, Myers).

The International Indigenous RPL Practitioner Manual

NEEDS EMPOWERMENT

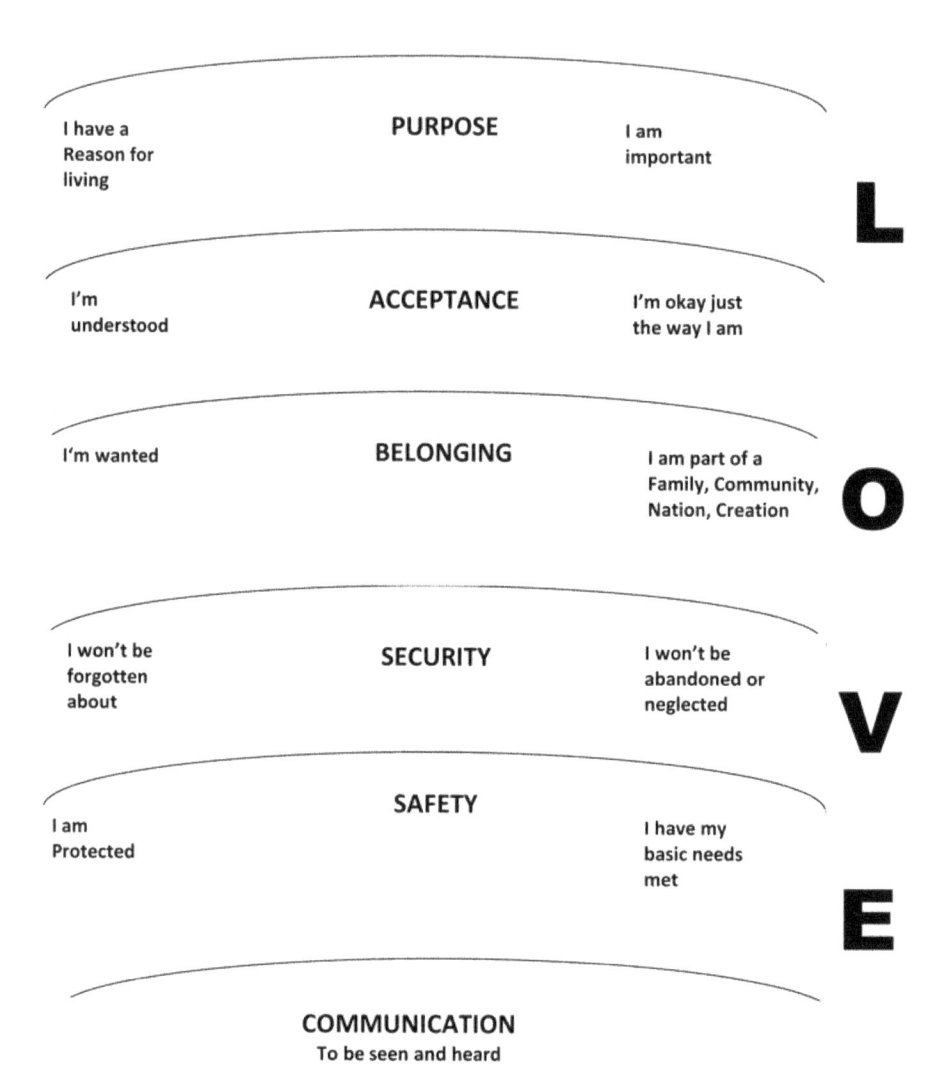

	PURPOSE	
I have a Reason for living		I am important

	ACCEPTANCE	
I'm understood		I'm okay just the way I am

	BELONGING	
I'm wanted		I am part of a Family, Community, Nation, Creation

	SECURITY	
I won't be forgotten about		I won't be abandoned or neglected

	SAFETY	
I am Protected		I have my basic needs met

COMMUNICATION
To be seen and heard

L O V E

MODULE IV

Haudenosaunee Longhouse
The Haudenosaunee Learner

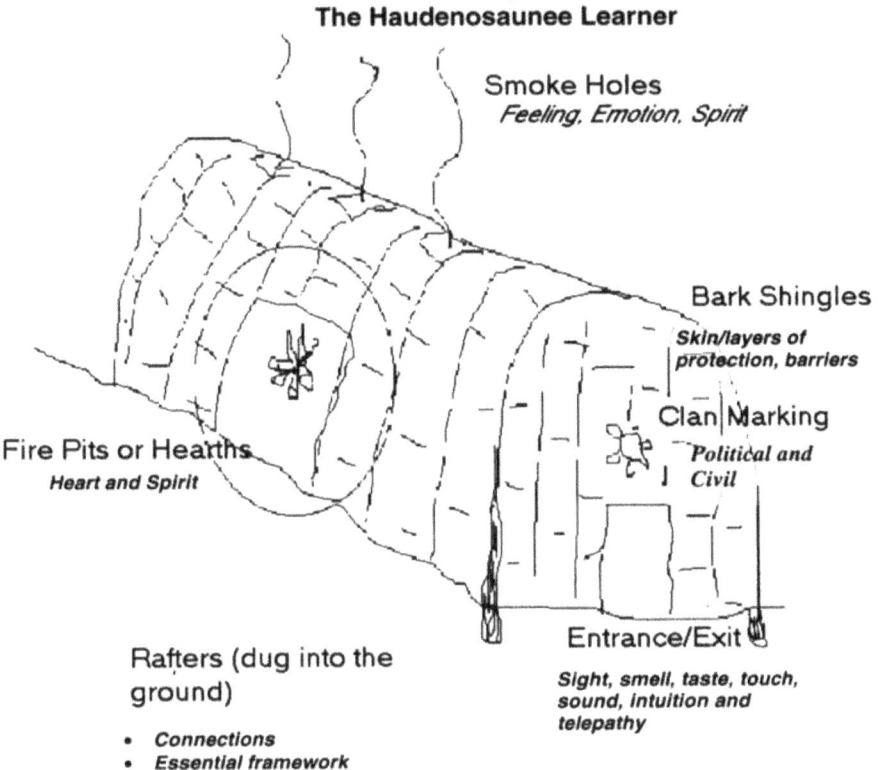

Smoke Holes
Feeling, Emotion, Spirit

Bark Shingles
Skin/layers of protection, barriers

Clan Marking
Political and Civil

Fire Pits or Hearths
Heart and Spirit

Entrance/Exit
Sight, smell, taste, touch, sound, intuition and telepathy

Rafters (dug into the ground)
- Connections
- Essential framework
- Stability

PHYSICAL

- Relaxation (rest/leisure)
- Exercise
- Diet
- Health
- Employment (workload/job hours)

The Rafters

The rafters, which are the frame and essential structure of the longhouse, represent our spine and ribcage. These rafters of our individual longhouse are also representative of the segments and stages in our life. The rafters can be strong or weak depending on the experiences an individual has encountered and the work one puts into it throughout their life. This is our house where all experiences and learning, both positive and negative are stored.

If each rafter is representative of some aspect of our lives, in theory it can be understood that all individuals would have at least eight essential rafters, beginning with the *self, family, clan (extended family), community, nation, confederacy, Creation, and universe.* These eight rafters represent our significant relationships within each life stage and the experiences and learning that we gain through these relationships.

In making PLA and portfolio development relevant to Haudenosaunee adult learners, it is important to explore these eight segments or rafters in order to begin to document their accumulated learning, skills, and knowledge.

When thinking about the teachings of the eight life stages *(infant, toddler, child, youth or adolescent, adult, parent, grandparent and elder)* and the eight rafters, what is recognized is that regardless of where we are in the human life cycle, we can explore our individual learning through the experience of our relationships to the family, clan, community, nation, confederacy, Creation, and universe.

Finally, in observation of the construction of the traditional Haudenosaunee Longhouse, it is important to note that each rafter was dug into the earth our mother for stability. They also reach into the sky creating a dome shape. This is symbolic not only of our connection as Haudenosaunee people to Mother Earth and the sky world, encompassing all of Creation, but it reminds us of the life cycle itself. All things come from the earth and so must return, although our spirit is thought to continue on. It also serves as a symbol of the duality of all things in which we must find balance. This is demonstrated throughout the Creation story, beginning with the twin brothers.

Bark Shingles

The shingles of the longhouse like our skin are a form of protection. If we have endured many powerful storms, we develop coping mechanisms to protect ourselves. These may also be viewed as an external barrier that individuals create in relation to the experiences they have encountered, both positive and negative.

MODULE IV

Entrance/Exit

The entrance/exit is the place where all experiences come into the longhouse. This includes what we experience through our senses: sight, smell, taste, touch, and sound. Intuition and telepathy (creativity) are also considered in the Haudenosaunee world view. Intuition, telepathy, and dreams are considered the language of the spirit or our inner consciousness.

MENTAL

- Social/governing structure
- Culture/heritage
- Community
- Role models
- Hobbies and special interests
- Relationships (interpersonal and intrapersonal)

Clan Markings

The clan marking that would appear over the entrance/exit of the longhouse, indicating the clan of the family in residence is symbolic of our political or civil responsibilities, specifically as outlined in the Kaianerekowa (Great Law of Peace). As Haudenosaunee people, the Great Law outlines our roles and responsibilities in life to our families, our communities, and ourselves. The three guiding principles of the Great Law are peace, power, and the Good Mind, also defining some of the characteristics of the individual.

SPIRITUAL

- Humility
- Guidance
- Support
- Serenity
- Love
- Inner strength
- Meditation

Fire Pits or Hearths

Within the longhouse fire pits are used for cooking, lighting, and warming the inside of the house. Metaphorically, the fire is our heart and spirit. The experiences we gain through our relationships to family, friends, and ultimately all of Creation are fuel for the fire. Our individual learning can make that spirit bright and strong. Experiences thought to be negative may dampen the fire, making it vulnerable. It is important to note that the way we respond to different experiences and the influences around us are reflected in how we feel about ourselves individually (learner self-esteem).

EMOTIONAL

- Feelings
- Self
- Life
- Skills and knowledge
- Personal issues
- Satisfaction (employment, personal, etc.)

Smoke Holes

The smoke hole is essentially the chimney. It allows smoke to escape from the longhouse. Our experiences generate feelings and emotions or energy which radiate out from our bodies, like the smoke rises from the longhouse. In a continuous cycle our experiences generate learning and feelings or emotions, which are released and create new relationships, experiences, and learning. The PLA portfolio process works to generate positive relationships, experiences, and learning.

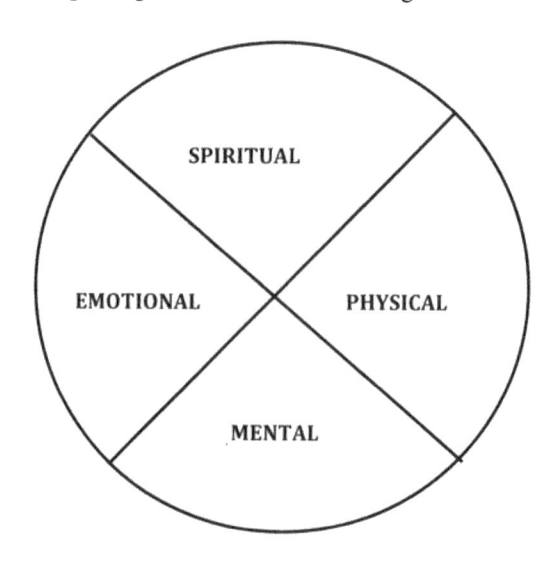

MODULE IV

EIGHT RAFTERS OF THE LONGHOUSE

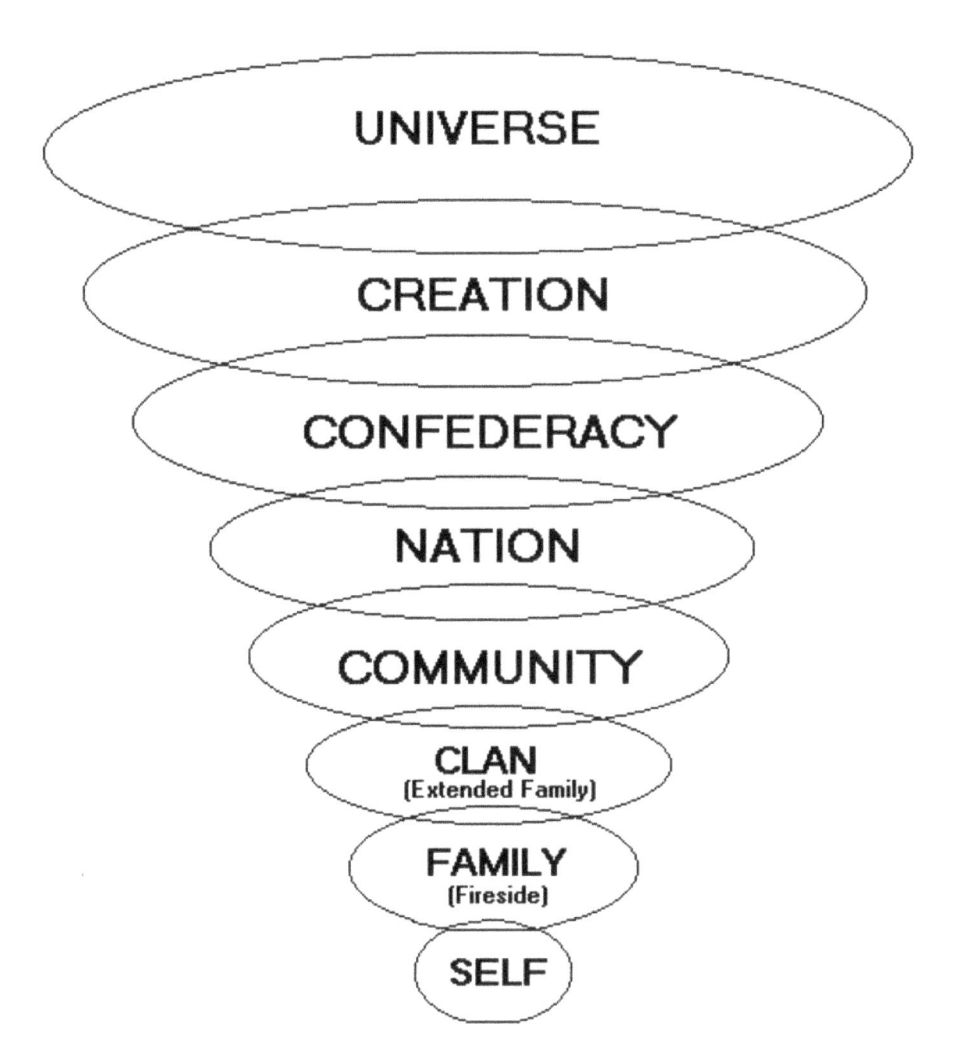

- UNIVERSE
- CREATION
- CONFEDERACY
- NATION
- COMMUNITY
- CLAN (Extended Family)
- FAMILY (Fireside)
- SELF

Represents a Spiral of Learning Reflection

DISCUSSION ON RELATIONSHIPS

Using the eight rafters (self, family, clan, community, nation, confederacy, Creation, and universe), the learner is guided through a process, which encourages the exploration of relationships to identify learning. Relationships are a key component of learning and accumulating life experiences, knowledge, and skills. For instance, you know who you are based on your relationship to family.

As an individual grows from infancy to adulthood their relationships grow as well. An infant is first associated with their immediate family unit or fireside family, and as they mature begins to develop relationships with grandparents, aunties, uncles, for example, or their clan (extended family). When a child becomes school-aged, they are exposed to community and society at large. This is the natural process that occurs as an individual moves through the eight life stages, ever expanding their relationships extending to Creation and the universe.

> "This learning process occurs in a spiral that supports and promotes the development of a greater consciousness and a deep understanding of one's self and the total environment."
>
> (Hill, 1999: 28)

In order to demonstrate the extension of relationships to Creation and beyond, take for instance "The Three Sisters," a common Haudenosaunee cultural reference to corn, beans, and squash. By using the term sisters, what is implied is a kinship with non-human elements. What is understood then is that these entities are to be viewed and treated with the same respect accorded or extended to family. Kinship relations can be found throughout Haudenosaunee culture and contribute to our way of relating and viewing the world, Creation, and the universe. Other examples are Mother Earth, Grandmother Moon, Elder Brother Sun, Grandfather Thunder, etc.

All things in Creation and the universe are related and interconnected. The Ohenton Karihwatehkwen (the words that come before all else), creates awareness for Haudenosaunee people of their relationship to all things in Creation and the universe, and as with any relationship comes responsibility. Our responsibility is to live in peaceful or respectful co-existence or harmony with all things. Harmony being recognition that all

MODULE IV

things have a purpose, which contributes to the overall continuation of Creation. This notion of harmony, which exists in Haudenosaunee philosophy, is also referred to as the "Good Mind." The Good Mind acknowledges the integrity and autonomy of all relationships.

As learners are challenged throughout the PLA portfolio process to reflect on their relationship to self, family, clan, community, nation, confederacy, Creation, and universe, they come to understand that each relationship is a valuable gift that stimulates learning.

FACILITATOR REFLECTIONS/NOTES

The facilitator is encouraged to become the lead participant in the group by transferring responsibility, decision-making, and problem-solving over to the group as a whole. Active participation in activities leading up to portfolio items is essential in establishing a sense of equality between the facilitator and learners. The facilitator's involvement in these activities must include a willingness to share some of their own experiences to demonstrate and role model how learning opportunities exist in all life experiences, including those experiences that may be considered negative or hurtful. Remember there are no bad opportunities to learn. In fact, hurtful experiences often plant the seed for personal development and growth if one is trained to identify that learning has occurred.

> "Despite the maps, charts, formulas, verbs, stories and books, I have really had nothing to teach, for my students really only have themselves to learn, and I know it takes the whole world to tell you who you are."
>
> (Canfield and Hanson, 2002: 203)

Learners may initially look to the facilitator for guidance, that is, what behaviour is accepted, how to address difficult issues in a respectful way, active listening, how to offer positive feedback and encouragement, how to acknowledge new ideas, etc. You are the role model for the skills of empowerment. Be aware of the energy and messages you are putting out there.

Facilitators may consider the following questions to help evaluate their role as a lead participant within the group:

- Have the learners developed respect and trust in each other?

- Have learners demonstrated willingness to change/progress?
- Are learners participating, cooperating, and sharing responsibilities?
- Are opportunities for success and empowerment being created?
- Is the best expected of each learner?
- Did learners have the opportunity to practice new skills?
- Are learners reflecting on the process and offering feedback?
- Are learners becoming self-directed (making their studies relevant to their interests, needs, goals, learning, skills, and knowledge)?

The facilitator is responsible for tracking the growth of learners. The following list provides signs of empowered learners:

- Learners participate in ongoing consultation with the facilitator and offer constructive/reflective feedback on the process.
- Learners participate in group decision-making and problem-solving.
- Learners identify and respect diversity (multiculturalism).
- Learners are experiencing skills development (communications, leadership, decision-making, group dynamics, etc.).
- Learners demonstrate an understanding of self and others.
- Learners have an awareness of community resources and can access these resources.
- Learners demonstrate enthusiasm and a belief in their own potential.
- Learners celebrate their identity as Indigenous people.

Facilitators may also watch for physical changes or signs of empowerment. For instance, learners may take more pride in their personal appearance or walk more confidently.

Skills of Empowerment:

- Self-esteem
- Assertiveness
- Communications
- Decision-making
- Leadership
- Collaboration
- Critical thinking
- Conflict Management
- Problem-solving
- Creative thinking
- Information gathering
- Healthy Risk-taking

MODULE IV

> **SPECIAL NOTE:**
>
> Finally, the process of exploring and documenting prior learning and life experiences with Indigenous adult learners may invoke or solicit emotions. The activities contained within the portfolio process challenge learners to observe, reflect on, and reframe personal issues of identity and self-worth and may reveal both personal and learning barriers. In light of this, facilitators utilizing the portfolio process are advised to have counseling services/referrals available or to have training/experience in the counseling field themselves.
>
> Just as important, facilitators are reminded that humour and laughter are integral to a healthy Indigenous identity and are known to release healing properties.

Learners should be encouraged to collect quotes, poems, etc., that inspire them. These items can be included throughout their portfolio.

RECOMMENDATIONS AND USE OF THE PORTFOLIO PROCESS

The PLA portfolio process was designed to accommodate adult literacy learners. The recommended duration of the program is 10 to 15 hours per week for a period of 10 to 12 weeks. The PLA portfolio process can also be adapted for other uses, including higher education and employment specific goals, for example.

The training program was modularized and outcomes based. There were eight modules, and each module was divided into three sections: activities, portfolio activities, and strategies for reflective thinking. Within each section there were sample activities intended to guide the process; however, there should be plenty of room for adding and/or deleting activities to ensure the facilitators' unique style and creativity are respected. As well, it allows for the specific needs of each learner within the group to be addressed in delivery, making it relevant and culturally appropriate.

The activities section offered suggested activities to build and maintain group cohesion, encourage sharing, display abilities, identify interests and strengths, as well as provide opportunities for learner empowerment. Learners are encouraged to facilitate team building or other activities they have learned or experienced in their lives and to document their leadership for their portfolio. The activities provided in each module come from a variety of sources and aid in the preparation of learners for the completion of portfolio activities.

Portfolio activities are the items that learners are required to complete through a variety of means to be inserted and organized into their master portfolio. Many portfolio items focus on and promote the documentation of life experiences and learning, skills and knowledge identification, goal setting, employability, specific and transferable skills, as well inspirational and cultural items that support a healthy sense of identity, purpose, and feeling of empowerment/belonging. By identifying and honouring the skills and knowledge of each learner, the facilitator and the group are truly acknowledging and honouring the spirit of that person.

The materials needed for the activities and portfolio items include the following: binders, dividers, clear plastic protector pages, and notebooks are the only additional required materials. Learners may work together to raise funds for any additional materials, supplies, or resources they feel would enhance their portfolios. Some learners may choose an electronic portfolio and only keep hard copies of important documents and support materials.

The involvement of elders should be considered and incorporated into the process as frequently as possible. Elders are not simply a cultural resource; they are rich in life experience and serve as role models and leaders in Indigenous communities.

OVERVIEW OF PORTFOLIO ITEMS

    Portfolio cover page
    Covering letter
    Resume
    List of references
    Tips for writing a covering letter
    Resume writing tips

Self

    Autobiography
    Chronology or timeline
    My collage and commentary

MODULE IV

My name in print
My learning style
All about super me

Family (Fireside Family)

Introduction to my family
Family tree
Family story
Family related skills—Cultural knowledge

Clan (Extended Family)

Clanology (clan characteristics activity)
Generational knowledge and/or skill documentation (beading, leather work, hunting)—cultural fluency and ways of knowing
Hobbies/Special interests documentation

Community

Reference list of community services
Brief community profile
Tips for job hunting
Employment confirmation letters
Employment reference letters
Volunteer confirmation letters
Personal letters of reference
Awards, certificates, diplomas, and transcripts—examples of localized knowledge and skills related to land and region

Nation

Strengths inventory
Knowledge, skills, experience chart
National logo and commentary—how we celebrate, share, and express our national identity, our interactions, and communication with our sister communities, Native language

Confederacy

Employability skills document
Personal contract/philosophy/mission statement

The Great Law of Peace and the formation of the confederacy—our involvement with the communities of the Six Nations/Haudenosaunee

Creation

Goals paper (personal, professional, education and/or training)
Skills for the 21st century
My global perspective
Creation story—what does it teach us about relationships, ceremonies, and the origins of things?

Universe

My responsibilities—the next seven generations
Ohenton Karihwatehkwen (greetings to the natural world)
Inspirational items
Learners are encouraged to add photographs, samples of their work, and other items to provide a balance of direct and indirect evidence of their skills and knowledge as well as items that personalize their portfolio.

BIBLIOGRAPHY

Aboriginal Family Healing and Joint Steering Committee. "For Generations to Come: The Time is Now, A Strategy for Aboriginal Family Healing." Final Report, Prepared September 1993.

Antone, Miller, Myers. *The Power Within People, A Community Organizing Perspective*. Mr. Print: Belleville, Ontario 1986.

Bernard, Kavoukian, Lloyd, Studd, Tauer. *You've Got It—use It: Strategies and Programs that Empower Students at Risk to Stay in School*. Desktop Publishing: New York, Ontario, 1995.

Canfield and Hansen. *Chicken Soup for the Teachers Soul*. Health Communications Inc.: Deerfield Beach, Florida, 2002.

Cornelius, Carol. "The Thanksgiving Address, An Expression of Haudenosaunee World view." *Akwe:ko Journal*. New York, Fall 1992.

Day, Malcolm, and Paul Zakos. "Developing Benchmarks for Prior Learning Assessment and Recognition, Practitioner Perspectives." Canadian Association for Prior Learning Assessment, Tyendinaga Mohawk Territory, Ontario, 2000.

George, Priscilla. *Vision, Guiding Native Literacy*. Ningwakwe Learning Press: Owen Sound, Ontario 1997.

Haudenosaunee Environmental Task Force. *Words That Come Before All Else, Environmental Philosophies of the Haudensoaunee*. North American Travelling College: Cornwall Island, Ontario, 1999.

Hill, Diane, and Priscilla George. *Native Learning Styles: An Assessment Tool* Owen Sound, Ontario: Ningwakwe Learning Press, 1998.

Hill, Diane. Holistic Learning: "A Model of Education based on Aboriginal Cultural Philosophy." Unpublished M.A. Thesis Antigonish, N.S.: Saint Francis Xavier University, 1999.

Hill, Diane; Banakonda Bell; Lynn Wilson and Joy Chamberlain. "Aboriginal Access to Post-Secondary Education, Prior Learning Assessment and its use within Aboriginal Programs of Learning." Tyendinaga Mohawk Territory, Ontario: First Nations Technical Institute: Ontario, March 1995.

Mitchell, Mike. *Traditional Teachings*. North American Indian Travelling College: Cornwall Island, Ontario, 1984.

The Igloo of Life

BACKGROUND

The Igloo of Life was an important component of a federally funded, three-year project in Canada in partnership with Nunavut Arctic College (NAC), led by Jennifer Archer.

The project aimed to integrate RPL and portfolio development into adult basic education programming at the college. The project had three goals for adult learners

1. Experience a positive change in self-image and self-confidence
2. Increase literacy skills and
3. Set goals for education and employment

To construct a culturally respectful portfolio development process, NAC staff worked with Janice Brant of Tyendinaga Mohawk Territory and Diane Hill of Six Nations Mohawk Nation Grand River who willingly shared their expertise in the application of cultural teachings to the portfolio development process. Janice and Diane worked closely with the NAC staff to create a holistic portfolio process which would honour and respect Inuit culture and teachings. An extensive consultation process took place in the early stages of the project. Elders, adult educators, adult learners, and representatives from various community groups and organizations across Nunavut were all given opportunities to help shape the nature and direction of the portfolio process to ensure its connection to Inuit culture and communities. Extensive training in facilitation of the portfolio process also took place with adult educators in many communities. An RPL facilitator's guide was created and modified as a result of the various consultations that took place.

The holistic portfolio process that was created as a result of this project was grounded in Inuit traditions, knowledge, and values. It was based on a foundation supported by Inuit Quajimajatuqangit (world view) with the understanding that Inuit culture has its own knowledge systems and ways of sharing knowledge. It also acknowledges that within most Indigenous cultures the circle of learning is not simply cognitive but holistic, engaging one's spirits, hearts, minds, and bodies. As well the holistic portfolio process enables learners to explore their experiences within the context of shared culture, language, and history including the experience of colonization.

The curriculum for the portfolio development course consisted of twelve sections with each section providing participants the opportunity to explore different areas of life learning. One of the key elements of the course was the Igloo of Life, created by Meeka Arnakaq, an elder from the community of Pangnirtung. She worked as an adult educator at the Community Learning Centre in Pangnirtung and for many years facilitated personal development and healing workshops. Meeka and her sister Leena Evic prepared and translated some of her core teachings which were key parts of the portfolio development course at NAC.

The Igloo of Life is a self-assessment tool created by Meeka as a model for personal development that uses igloo blocks to represent the building blocks of a whole, healthy person. Meeka suggests exploring each block sequentially, according to the interests and pace of the learning group. The igloo is made up of fifteen blocks. Each block represents an aspect of the self, working together as a whole, healthy, human being. Learners are introduced to the Igloo of Life by exploring how the self is like an igloo. They are invited to read the titles of each block together and then reflect on the first block, writing their ideas in a booklet. The titles for each block include, Knowing Yourself Clearly; Learning About Yourself; Self-Discipline and Personal Empowerment; Protecting

MODULE IV

Yourself; Practising Patience; Understanding Yourself; Telling Your Own Story; Viewing Yourself; Love Yourself; Gratitude; Empowering Yourself; Managing Your Own Life; Be Your Own Best Friend; Believe in Yourself; Having Integrity.

At the end of each session learners are invited to reflect on the next block in the sequence, beginning with the first block, "Knowing Yourself Clearly." Meeka encourages learners to share what they know about how igloos are built; it takes many snow blocks to make a strong shelter. The snow blocks must have enough depth; if the snow is not hard enough, it can be improved by stamping it down. An igloo must be built on a strong foundation; otherwise it will not be a good shelter. These various qualities are compared to the challenges faced by human beings in their life journey in terms of understanding the many aspects of ourselves: continuing to develop and celebrate all of our gifts, strengthening ourselves by learning new skills and knowledge, and also strengthening our personal foundations by learning about and valuing ourselves.

Starting with block one, Meeka has written descriptions for each block, and learners are asked to review the commentary for the first block and record their thoughts in writing. Each member of the group is asked to share some of their thoughts about the block. Page 123 illustrates the Igloo of Life with the various block numbers and topics.

The commentary for block one, "Knowing Yourself Clearly," is as follows: "The first important step toward personal growth is to explore ourselves and our experiences. Do we know who we really are, where we come from, and what our core personal values are based on? Are our values playing a big role in creating stability in our lives? Our knowledge about ourselves starts from our cultural background and community. What does your cultural background and community mean to you?"

Learners are asked to explore their life experiences in order to recognize how much they have learned and how much they know and can do. For block one they are asked to write or draw one or two things that they know about themselves. For example, they could record a value they hold strongly or a personal quality they value about themselves.

LEARNER FEEDBACK

As part of the course evaluation process learners were asked about the impact that the portfolio development process had on them with regard to what they learned about themselves:

"This has really taught me about myself. I've begun to realize who I am and who I want to be."

"I have learned to love myself more."

"I have learned a lot about myself that I never saw. I never knew what kind of a person I was. It made me feel really good about myself, and that I can help others too."

"I realize I have more knowledge to pass on now than I did before the program."

"It was good to learn about how I am able to accept what I have gone though in my life and what I am still going to face."

"I appreciate the course. It was healing, and it helped me a lot."

"If you would take this course, you would start seeing yourself."

"I've learned that I am really somebody."

SUMMARY

This section of the International Indigenous RPL Practitioner manual is based on materials taken from the portfolio development facilitator's guide created by Nunavut Arctic College as part of the implementation of the three-year (2007–2010) project funded by the Government of Canada. More detailed information on the project, especially the culturally based portfolio development process and the Igloo of Life created by Meeka Arnakaq is available on a CD and in printed format. Three members of the board of directors of the Collective, Banakonda Kennedy-Kish Bell, Mark Gallupe, and Paul Zakos, were part of the team that helped implement the three-year project.

MODULE IV

The Igloo of Life

By Meeka Arnakaq

- Having Integrity
- Manage Your Own Life
- Be Your Own Best Friend
- Believe In Yourself
- Love Yourself
- Gratitude
- Empowering Yourself
- Practicing Patience
- Understanding Yourself
- Telling Your Own Story
- Viewing Yourself
- Knowing Yourself Clearly
- Learning About Yourself
- Self-discipline and Personal Empowerment
- Protecting Yourself

MODULE V

Indigenous Knowledge and Quality Assurance

Assessing Your Institution or Program's Level of Integration of Indigenous Knowledge Using the Benchmarks of Best Practice Developed by the Collective

Introduction

This module identifies a set of benchmarks of quality assurance for consideration by institutions and programs delivering educational services to Indigenous learners and their communities. It outlines a self-assessment process that can be used by educational institutions to determine their effectiveness in serving Indigenous learners. The informal assessment process is evidence-based and focused on the critical roles and responsibilities of those delivering the educational activities. The end result is the creation of an institutional (or program) portfolio identifying strengths and gaps in services.

Module Outcomes

Upon successful completion of this module, participants should be able to:

- Explain the importance of incorporating Indigenous knowledge and customs into the policies and procedures of educational systems, individual institutions, and programs.
- List and describe the four principles that constitute a holistic framework for Indigenous educational endeavours.
- Identify ways in which the institutional self-assessment process can help educational systems and institutions ensure that their policies and programs reflect and respect Indigenous teachings and customs.

Context for the Institutional Self-Evaluation Process
— *Sharon Hobenshield*

The failure to recognize the inherent rights of Indigenous people is a global issue perpetuated by systemic oppression, fostered by beliefs and values that privilege certain ways of thinking and being over others. Eurocentric thinking has created a gap in the attainment of education with Indigenous people being placed at the lower echelons worldwide. To redress this glaring inequity, organizations and systems will need to be more open, respectful, and inclusive of Indigenous belief systems and world views.

The vision of the International Indigenous RPL Collective includes actively supporting the rights of Indigenous nations as full partners in the societies in which they live. Integral to this belief is the formal recognition of Indigenous ways of knowing across educational systems and within educational institutions. Along with this acknowledgement is the recognition and acceptance of the historical implications of colonization. The Collective advocates for and is committed to, building authentic relationships with the Indigenous people and recognizes that distinctions exist among various nations, communities, and families in relation to geographical location, experiences, cultural traditions, and knowledge structures.

The relationship building process is a component of a strategy which is focused on the integration of Indigenous perspectives both in educational systems and within individual institutions. Relationship building must be flexible, non-prescriptive, and tailored to fit the circumstances and the context of the Indigenous nation and its location in each country and community. Interactions between institutions and Indigenous nations and their communities should be culturally respectful, transparent, and collaborative.

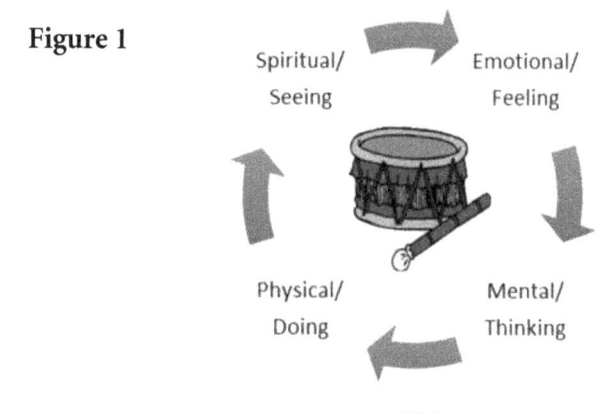

Figure 1

Spiritual/Seeing → Emotional/Feeling → Mental/Thinking → Physical/Doing

MODULE V

The holistic approach as illustrated in Figure One provides a framework to help you determine your institution or organization's current relationship with Indigenous teachings, customs, and support services to learners.

The rating scale which follows has been created to assist you to informally assess your organization's services to Indigenous learners along four dimensions related to Indigenous knowledge, structures, and support services. The four dimensions are emotional/feeling, mental/thinking, physical/doing, and spiritual/seeing.

Each of the categories includes a description of the principles and a set of performance criteria to guide the informal assessment of your organization's current relationship with the Indigenous people in your area.

The four dimensions are viewed as being cyclical and interconnected rather than as separate and fragmented parts. As you work through each of the four principles and reflect on your current practices, our hope is that you will identify areas of strength and gaps needing to be filled. Our intent is that this activity will be productive and worthwhile, leading to a continuous improvement process in the way your services are offered to Indigenous learners and their communities.

Introduction to the Institutional Self-Assessment Process

The goal of this module is to identify and share a set of practices for consideration by educational systems and institutions serving Indigenous learners. These practices have been implemented by Indigenous educators in higher education. They are offered in the spirit of cooperation to those seeking guidance and inspiration in their work with Indigenous learners and their communities. Our hope is that this work will serve as a practical tool which helps institutions to reflect on their strengths and identify gaps in their services to Indigenous learners as they move toward the integration of Indigenous knowledge within their organizations. Our intent is that this process will assist you to ensure that Indigenous knowledge becomes an integral and permanent component of the ideological and political fabric of your organization.

The self-evaluation process is built around a holistic framework which consists of four dimensions. They are **emotional**, **mental**, **physical,** and **spiritual** elements. We view the integration of feeling, thinking, doing, and seeing as key aspects of a principled approach which helps to govern our actions and guide our relationships. These principles reflect an approach to learning that respects and honours the heart, mind, and spirit. The drum is used as a metaphor and as a universal symbol to assist in putting in place a reflective process that leads to action. The drum is considered to be the heartbeat of Mother Earth for Indigenous peoples living on Turtle Island. It is alive and reinforces that all things have spirit and energy. The recognition of this interconnectedness is what makes us whole. There is an understanding that the world and all of Creation are in a constant state of learning.

Each Indigenous tribe, nation, and clan has its own unique teachings and protocols for the construction and use of the drum, and this reflects the diversity among Indigenous people around the world. In this instance, the drum can be seen as a metaphor that helps us to focus our attention and efforts in an Indigenous approach to learning.

Performing the Informal Institutional Self-Assessment

This section outlines the basic steps and principles involved in assessing your institution's level of integration of Indigenous knowledge and customs. The four principles listed in the self-assessment scale along with their accompanying performance criteria are intended to help guide you as you conduct the assessment. Prior to engaging in the assessment, it is worthwhile to consider the way in which you can best accomplish the task. We strongly suggest that you create a team with membership from across various departments, particularly focusing on those persons who have prior experience with any of the categories outlined on the self-assessment scale. This approach is more objective and preferable to having one individual perform the entire assessment.

Once you have decided on the composition of the assessment team, carefully review the four principles and the performance indicators that exemplify their application to your organization. Record what you think is the present level of performance at your institution. Place a mark in the column Y (Yes), N (No), or UD (Under Development) that best describes your institution's current performance in that area. In the next column make note of the unit or person responsible for the principle that is being assessed and the name of the person in charge of the unit. Make notes of

MODULE V

possible sources of documentation in the right-hand (Evidence) column. List particular items such as mission statements, recruitment and instructional materials, websites, newspaper articles, policy statements, and projects which can be used to provide concrete evidence of your institution's level of integration of Indigenous knowledge and customs.

Upon completion of the informal institutional self-assessment, it is a good idea to prepare a report on your findings.

PROPOSED DEVELOPMENTS/IMPROVEMENTS ARISING OUT OF PROCESS (RECOMMENDATIONS)
(See figure below)

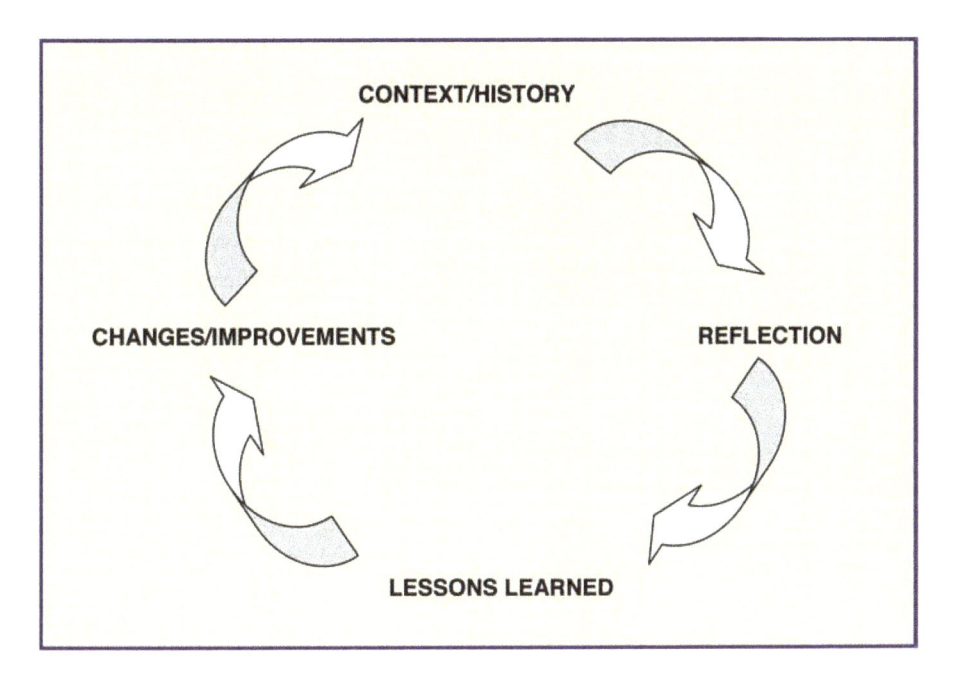

[Figure: A cyclical diagram with four stages connected by arrows in a circle: CONTEXT/HISTORY → REFLECTION → LESSONS LEARNED → CHANGES/IMPROVEMENTS → (back to CONTEXT/HISTORY)]

Preparing a Final Report—Suggested Framework

Upon completion of the informal institutional self-assessment, it may be useful to prepare a final report which provides a context for the self-assessment. We have prepared an outline to assist you with the report (Appendix D). The outline includes an institutional profile, reflective questions, and lessons learned.

Institutional/Organizational Informal Self-Assessment—Roles and Responsibilities Related to Implementing Culturally Respectful Indigenous Knowledge Systems and Programs

In the Indigenous paradigm, knowledge is relational, holistic, and inclusive of the spiritual, emotional, intellectual, and physical realms.

1. PRINCIPLE – EMOTIONAL/FEELING

It is essential that institutions and organizations create ongoing opportunities for truth telling, witnessing and learning, fostering emotional connections to invoke the process of decolonization. Elders often refer to the longest learning journey being the one from your head to your heart, suggesting that both are necessary for knowing and being in the world. In this context, knowledge creation is not simply a cognitive endeavor but one that also engages emotion and feeling from a heart place.

Y = Yes
N = No
UD = Under Development

ROLES, RESPONSIBILITES

PERFORMANCE INDICATORS	Y	N	UD	UNIT/PERSON RESPONSIBLE	EVIDENCE
• Create sustainable relationships with local Indigenous communities, organizations.					
• Employ Elders and Traditional Knowledge Keepers					
• Use local protocols, ceremonies and songs embedded throughout under the direction of the local Indigenous communities.					
• Organize regular meetings between senior management of institution and local Indigenous leadership.					
• Create structures, processes which enable students, staff to have access to Elders, Traditional Knowledge Keepers.					
• Implement agreements that honor mutual partnerships which uphold local knowledge and traditions.					

MODULE V

2. PRINCIPLE – MENTAL/THINKING

Indigenous knowledge is fluid, holistic and informed by language, ancestors, and lived experience on the land and enacting ceremony. It is a value-based approach to learning and living: values that come from family, culture, and community. The way of thinking and interpreting environments is therefore more intuitive in nature than analytical.

ROLES, RESPONSIBILITES

Y = Yes
N = No
UD = Under Development

PERFORMANCE INDICATORS	Y	N	UD	UNIT/PERSON RESPONSIBLE	EVIDENCE
• Design curriculum, educational delivery and evaluation that includes history of local Indigenous people and their relationship to the area, region.					
• Recognize oral nature of Indigenous cultures.					
• Create governance structure for the organization which ensures representation and participation of Indigenous peoples.					
• Promote Indigenous nations, groups as full-partners in policy, planning, delivery and evaluation.					

3. PRINCIPLE – PHYSICAL/DOING

Relationality is at the core of Indigenous knowledge systems. Relations within cultures, traditions, kinship groups, spirituality and ceremony provide the foundation for our physical existence and knowledge. There is a direct correlation between how we come to know through the continual regeneration among all these relations and our responsibility to disseminate this knowledge in a good way for future generations.

ROLES, RESPONSIBILITES

Y = Yes
N = No
UD = Under Development

PERFORMANCE INDICATORS	Y	N	UD	UNIT/PERSON RESPONSIBLE	EVIDENCE
• Implement collaborative approaches enabling collective consciousness-raising and social action.					
• Design processes, structures which ensure Indigenous people are part of management team, staff.					
• Implement learning series as part of the institution's professional development program.					
• Design hiring practices that include affirmative action.					

MODULE V

4. PRINCIPLE – SPIRITUAL/SEEING

Indigenous peoples knowledge is cumulative informed by history, ancestors, oral communication, practice and ongoing interactions with all things. Understanding is reinforced through ritual and spirituality. It is specific paradigm best described below:

> Aboriginal paradigms include ideas of constant flux, all existence consisting of energy waves/spirit, all things being animate, all existence being interrelated, creation/existence having to be renewed, space/place as an important referent, and language, songs, stories, and ceremonies as repositories for the knowledge that arise out of these paradigms. (Little Bear 2009, p. 8)

ROLES, RESPONSIBILITES

```
Y  = Yes
N  = No
UD = Under Development
```

PERFORMANCE INDICATORS	Y	N	UD	UNIT/PERSON RESPONSIBLE	EVIDENCE
• Create structures and processes that validate Indigenous ways of knowing and protect intellectual property rights.					
• Design spaces and places for ceremony.					
• Recognize ceremony as integral to learning.					
• Recognize and use local Indigenous language.					
• Develop ethical guidelines for use of Indigenous knowledge.					
• Arrange for people within organization to participate in ceremony on a regular basis.					
• Design institutional signage (marketing and promotion) that reflects local language.					
• Offer local language classes.					

The International Indigenous RPL Practitioner Manual

Summary

This manual is dedicated to Indigenous peoples around the world. Its content is intended to enable educational systems, individual institutions, and community-based organizations to evaluate their services to Indigenous adult learners and their communities and to assess the extent to which they embrace culturally respectful approaches to the delivery of learning to Indigenous peoples. The process highlights adult friendly policies and practices that formally recognize Indigenous knowledge using a variety of assessment approaches to identify, articulate, and validate Indigenous ways of knowing. Although this work focuses mainly on the needs of Indigenous adults and their communities, many of the principles and processes apply to children and youth.

The Collective firmly believes that the development of guidelines for International Indigenous RPL practice for individuals and institutions is a necessary strategy that can make an important contribution to the creation of a set of international best practices for the RPL. We are working toward the development of benchmarks and performance criteria that reflect the diversity of Indigenous language and customs and which serve as the foundation for a quality assurance process that places respect for Indigenous knowledge and languages and the needs of Indigenous communities at the centre of all endeavours relating to the learning needs of Indigenous peoples.

Internationally, there is a need to continue to develop strategies and processes that work toward the recognition of the legitimacy of Indigenous teachings, which recognize the diversity of Indigenous languages, customs, and community needs. Much of RPL practice globally, does not acknowledge the significance of traditional knowledge and cultural teachings. Generally RPL practice is characterized by guidelines and principles which are narrow and technical, focusing almost exclusively on employment skills and competencies to the exclusion of the diverse languages and cultures of Indigenous peoples throughout the world. We would like also to point out that not all cultures are driven by the need to compete in the global marketplace and that Indigenous knowledge and ways of knowing may also enhance employability and social mobility both within the mainstream and in Indigenous communities. It is in this context that a

MODULE V

current priority for Indigenous communities, in addition to employability skills, is the recognition, maintenance, and strengthening of their language and culture.

Although mainstream thinking often implies that non-industrialized societies might be regarded as, vulnerable or disadvantaged, our belief is that industrialized nations might benefit from Indigenous values, beliefs, and practices especially in the fields of ecology, health care, and human relations. For example in Chile, the Mapuche people have developed intercultural health programs in collaboration with the Chilean Ministry of Health in some urban areas. In these programs the Machi, a spiritual and physical healer, regularly consults with clients regarding a variety of health issues. This program is open to both Indigenous and non-Indigenous community members with the full support of the Chilean Ministry of Health.

Any guidelines or policies related to Indigenous knowledge and customs must contribute to the creation of a set of principles which define learning in a broad and flexible way and include the ethical, connotative, and cultural domains of learning that are of critical importance to Indigenous communities. They must also recognize the unique social structure of Indigenous communities and the key role this structure plays in maintaining and sustaining lifelong learning, for example, the unique functions and contributions of elders in the stability and development of healthy and vibrant Indigenous communities. The skills and knowledge of elders and other community leaders are not acknowledged by mainstream approaches. Thus financial compensation and formal recognition are virtually non-existent, and the significance of elders to the lives of individuals, communities, and indeed the entire society is often ignored or underestimated. Employability and the qualities and characteristics of healthy communities are often viewed through a very narrow lens in mainstream society.

The vision, mission, and objectives of the Collective (Appendix C) are consistent with the context of Articles 13 and 14 of the UN Declaration on the Rights of Indigenous Peoples (Appendix A) and the aims and objectives of the World Indigenous Nations Higher Education Consortium (WIN-HEC, Appendix B). They advocate for recognition of the legitimacy of Indigenous languages, cultures, and ways of knowing and aim to nurture and strengthen the desire of Indigenous people to assume their rightful places as full partners in the societies in which they live.

The Collective believes that culturally respectful approaches to learning, including the recognition, validation, and accreditation of learning, enables Indigenous peoples to make informed choices related to improving their quality of life and standard of living. It also advocates for formal recognition of Indigenous ways of knowing which support and respect traditional knowledge, strengthen language, culture, and self-determination. Collaboration with key stakeholders from the public and private sector is essential in order to create institutions and practices that respect the validity and credibility of Indigenous knowledge, cultural teachings, and languages. Standards and methods of assessment should be developed and articulated by recognizing knowledge keepers from within Indigenous nations and cultures.

This manual and the work of the Collective are dedicated to the development of partnerships and trusting relationships with organizations, groups and individuals interested in collaborating to address the imbalances and inequities that currently characterize approaches to the creation, delivery, and evaluation of Indigenous knowledge and customs. We realize that the content and processes found in this manual are incomplete and evolving. We welcome feedback regarding possible options and strategies which would ensure that this work is strengthened and accurately reflects, in a meaningful way, Indigenous languages and cultures and the needs of Indigenous communities.

APPENDIX A

United Nations Declaration on the Rights of Indigenous Peoples

Article 13: Indigenous peoples have the right to revitalize, use, develop and transmit to future generations their histories, languages, oral traditions, philosophies, writing systems and literatures and to designate and retain their own names for communities, places and persons... States shall take effective measures to ensure that this right is protected.

Article 14: Indigenous peoples have the right to establish and control their educational systems and institutions providing education in their own languages, in a manner appropriate to their cultural methods of teaching and learning... States shall in conjunction with Indigenous peoples, take effective measures, in order for Indigenous individuals to an education in their own culture and provided in their own language.

APPENDIX B

World Indigenous Nations Higher Education Consortium (WINHEC)

- "We share the vision of Indigenous Peoples of the world united in the collective synergy of self-determination through control of higher education."
- "We are committed to building partnerships that restore and retain Indigenous spirituality, cultures and languages, homelands, social systems, economic systems and self-determination."
- "WINHEC provides an international forum and support for Indigenous Peoples to pursue common goals through higher education."

WINHEC Goals

- Accelerate the articulation of Indigenous epistemology (ways of knowing, education, philosophy, and research).
- Protect and enhance Indigenous spiritual beliefs, culture, and languages through higher education.
- Advance the social, economic, and political status of Indigenous peoples that contribute to the well-being of Indigenous communities through higher education.
- Create an accreditation body for Indigenous education initiatives and systems that identify common criteria, practices, and principles by which Indigenous peoples live.
- Recognize the significance of Indigenous education.

The International Indigenous RPL Practitioner Manual

- Create a global network for sharing knowledge through exchange forums and state of the art technology.
- Recognize the educational rights of Indigenous peoples.

APPENDIX C

The International Indigenous RPL Collective

Vision

The International Indigenous RPL Collective recognizes values and gives vision (voice) and legitimacy to Indigenous languages, cultures, and ways of knowing. It is inclusive, reflecting the needs, values, and wishes of diverse peoples. It nurtures and strengthens their desire to assume their rightful place as full partners in the societies in which they live.

The Collective believes that culturally respectful approaches to learning enable Indigenous peoples to make informed choices related to improving their quality of life, standard of living, and taking charge of their own destiny.

Mission

Working toward the creation of Indigenous controlled institutions of higher learning, the Collective aims to influence key policy decisions related to education and learning initiatives of governments and educational systems. It advocates for formal recognition of Indigenous ways of knowing which support and respect traditional knowledge, strengthen language, culture, and self-determination. It works cooperatively with its members and key stakeholders, from public and private sector, to create institutions and practices which respect the validity and credibility of Indigenous knowledge, cultural teachings, and languages. Standards and methods of assessment are developed and articulated by recognizing knowledge keepers from within the Collective.

Objectives

The International Indigenous RPLC promotes culturally based RPL and adult learning practices which:

1. Enhance, safeguard, and validate Indigenous languages, cultures, and ways of knowing.
2. Identify community strengths, resources, and needs.
3. Support collaborative approaches enabling collective consciousness raising and social action.
4. Strengthen self-confidence, self-reliance, and community capacity for self-determination.
5. Promote Indigenous nations and groups as full partners in educational policy, planning, delivery, and evaluation.
6. Create international Indigenous benchmarks of best practice for RPL within an integrated framework of culturally respectful adult learning principles and practices.
7. Support cooperative approaches to culturally based holistic learning.
8. Disseminate best practices and discover new practices.
9. Host regular gatherings of members and other interested stakeholder groups, organizations, and individuals.

APPENDIX D

Serving Indigenous Learners and Their Communities—Institutional/Organizational Informal Self-Assessment Preparing a Final Report

This section is intended to provide your institution with an outline to assist with the preparation of a final report upon completion of the informal institutional self-assessment process.

Institutional Profile

- History
- Demographics
- Indigenous learning approaches

Reflective Questions

1. What changes do you hope to make and what will be the implications for:
   - the organization
   - Indigenous learners
   - Indigenous community?

   Do you have any fears or concerns about the Institutional self-assessment process?

2. Have you identified any obstacles you think you will need to overcome?

3. What strategies and/or resources might contribute to a successful outcome?

Lessons Learned

1. What have you learned from the completing the institutional self-assessment?
2. How has the way in which you provide services to Indigenous learners and their community changed for the better?
3. What evidence do you have that this is the case?
4. Were you able to identify existing strengths in your services to Indigenous learners and their communities?
5. Did you uncover any major gaps in services to Indigenous learners and their communities?
6. How will you be able to use the results of the self-assessment to set priorities for further action?
7. Have you thought what the next steps in this process might be?

CPSIA information can be obtained
at www.ICGtesting.com
Printed in the USA
BVHW050406020821
612954BV00002B/3